THE BIG BOOK OF INTERNET ANSWERS

Your complete guide to trouble-free Net access

**Modems • Email
Web sites • Newsgroups
FTP • HTML • Glossary**

Published by Paragon Publishing Ltd
Paragon House, St Peter's Road,
Bournemouth, UK BH1 2JS
Tel: 01202 299900
Fax: 01202 299955
http://www.paragon.co.uk

Managing Editor: Geoff Harris
Contributors: Clive Parker, Paul Winslow, New
Media in Business Ltd (http://www.nmib.com)
Designer: Jane Evans
Production: Steve Hill, Jo Cole
Printed by: Mackays of Chatham plc
Published by: Paragon Publishing Ltd

CONTENTS

GETTING ONLINE

Connecting to the Internet has never been easier, but many of us suffer teething troubles when we first start out. From choosing the correct hardware to disconnecting from the Net, we show you how to sort out some common problems

ROUGH GUIDE

Q

I want to access the Internet for both recreational and business-related reasons. I have three main areas of uncertainty upon which I would appreciate your views.

The first is hardware. The Rough Guide book recommends the following specifications for efficient Internet operation: a Pentium with 16Mb of RAM, a 1 Gigabyte hard drive, a 32-bit sound card, a quad-speed CD-ROM drive, a 15-inch monitor as a minimum and a 56kbps modem. Is this information still relevant or have the specifications changed in the two years since the book was published?

Next, which operating system should I use? At the moment, I use Windows 95 at work – should I move to Windows 98 or should I get a PC with Windows 95?

Finally, I need reference sources. Other than *Practical Internet*, where can I find good advice on the best ways of maximising my effectiveness in using the Internet?

A

Hardware has moved on slightly since the specifications you quoted were relevant, although they could still be used as a bare minimum guide. If you are buying a new PC, you should choose a 200MHz Pentium II with 32Mb of RAM as a minimum. All PCs should come with a good multimedia set-up as standard, so you should get a 24-speed CD-ROM drive (or even DVD-ROM) and a good soundcard. A 15-inch monitor is still the minimum you should use, although it's a good idea to get a 17-inch monitor if you can afford it. A 56k modem is essential for fast Internet downloads and Web browsing.

By the time you read this, most new PCs will come with Windows 98 installed as standard. I have been using Windows 98 for a couple of months now, and I am very happy with the way it works. It has been designed to integrate Internet access more closely with the operating system, so it is more efficient at accessing the Internet than Windows 95. My only niggle with Windows 98 is the inability to disable the True Web Integration (TWI) feature first introduced with Internet Explorer 4 and the constant popping up of a dialogue box asking me if I want to join MSN every time I try to download email, even after selecting the 'Do Not Show This Message Again' box.

You can't go too far wrong with *Practical Internet* or our sister magazine *Internet Access Made Easy*. There are so many Internet books on the market, it's hard to choose a definitive reference. As a relative beginner, you should try Using The Internet (Fourth Edition) by Barbara Kasser. It's published by QUE for £27.49, ISBN 0-7897-1584-8.

TAKING IT TO TASK

Q

I have been using Internet Explorer 3.01 for a few months, and what I find useful is that when closing down the program, you are prompted with the question 'do you want to close your Internet connection?'

Please can you tell me how are you supposed to log off when using Netscape Navigator? I have recently tried out this software, and I can find no way to close my Internet connection without re-booting my system.

A

Windows 95 lets you disconnect from the Taskbar. When you are connected to the Internet, a connection icon appears in the bottom right-hand section of the Taskbar. It looks like two tiny computers. If you double-click on this icon, the connection status window opens. This has a Disconnect button. Simply click on this to disconnect from the Internet.

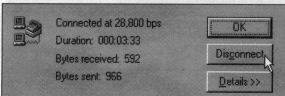

Connected at 28,800 bps
Duration: 000:03:33
Bytes received: 592
Bytes sent: 966

OK
Disconnect
Details >>

BT BOTHER

Q

In America you can pay as little as $12 a month for unlimited local phone time. I pay as much as 3.5 pence a minute for using the Net. I don't understand why we have a different billing system. Surely phone companies know how time consuming the Net is? My phone company didn't even know what IRC was. If you know of a phone company offering free local calls (any time or duration), I would be grateful to know about them.

A

BT has more than 95 per cent of the home telecoms market and can do pretty much what it likes. Some cable companies tried offering free calls at unsocial hours, but no longer appear to be so keen.

BT could go to a flat pricing model for local calls but it would quickly need more kit, because although the average voice call is just a few minutes regardless of cost (there's only so much to say once you leave adolescence behind), Net calls often consume hours – as you've found. With more people staying online for longer, BT needs more capacity, and it would rather make money than spend it. So basically, until someone else does it, BT won't move to flat pricing for local calls. And unless you have cable, no one else is going to run a wire to your house.

WWWHAT'S GOING ON?

Q Why do most Web sites have names beginning with www while a few don't? Why don't they all have www at the beginning?

A Excellent question. The name of a Web site (more technically, its Uniform Resource Locater, or URL) is a little more involved than it currently appears. Let's break down a fictitious site at Betanet, **www.betanet.com**.

In practice, this is read back to front. The most important bit is **com**, which defines the top level domain. The **betanet** part is normally the class B address, while the **www** is of interest only to the local servers at Betanet on which it resides.

When you type **www.betanet.com** into your browser, the Net routing system takes you as far as a DNS (domain name server) at betanet.com. This then says, 'oh yes, we've got a Web site called www here,' and gives you the relevant default page, usually index.htm or home.htm, depending on how it's been set up (but it could be anything including an active page with an asp filetype, for example). In fact, www has become a standard default Web site name because it means you only have to remember the middle bit. However, there's no reason it has to be www. A good example is **altavista.digital.com**, the famous search engine. If you type **www.digital.com** you get Digital's default company Web site. Since the services share a domain name – digital.com – they must have different server addresses locally. Other popular choices for server names include ftp (file transfer protocol) sites, which are often huge software archives.

GLOBAL MIX-UP

We use the Premium Line from BT, and we have listed the GlobalNet number as our Best Friend. Emailing my sister in South Africa is horrendously expensive. BT's pricing info tells us that daytime charges are 79.46 pence per minute; after 6pm it's 73.3 pence, and weekends cost 67.4 pence. There is a minimum charge of five minutes, thereafter they charge per second. I'm dreading the next bill coming in. Should I list GlobalNet as Friends and Family and the South African phone number as my Best Friend?

I think you are getting mixed up between email calls and normal phone calls. When you send an email to your sister in South Africa using your GlobalNet account, you are only calling the local [or LoCall] GlobalNet number. You are NOT making a phone call to South Africa every time you send an email message to your sister, you are instead making a local call charged at local rates.

The only time you would incur international call charges while connecting to the Internet would be if you used your modem to connect to a South African Internet provider using an international number. As you are using GlobalNet, I assume you are not doing this.

I have all my ISPs listed in my Friends and Family scheme for my modem line, it saves me a lot of money. You should only use the GlobalNet number as your Best Friend if your Internet connections are more expensive than your international phone calls.

CUT AND PASTE

Q I would like to know if it is possible for me to create an email message with a word processor and to then import that message into the email program?

A Yes. It is possible to create text messages in any word processor, then cut and paste them into your email software. To do this, you use the CTRL-C and CTRL-V cut and paste keyboard commands, or alternatively use the 'Copy' and 'Paste' commands found in the Edit menus of each program.

But the question is, why bother? It's just as easy, and certainly faster, to write your emails in the email program and then queue them ready for sending while you are working offline. You don't have to be connected to the Internet to compose your messages in your email program. You can write several then send them later. It's as simple and painless as that.

YOUR ISP

Internet service providers can cause a lot of headaches. From slow connection speeds, engaged tones and appalling technical support – you name it, we've heard about it. In this section, we deal with the most common ISP problems

BREATHE DEEPER

Q

I hope you can help me, because I don't know much about the Internet. I have an IBM ThinkPad 380ED with 166Mhz pentium, 48Mb RAM, 3Gb HD and 56k fax modem. My ISP is called Breathe, and I wondered if you can give me your opinion on its service. And can you tell me if a connection of 115,200bps is good or bad and where I can improve it?

A

I can't really give an opinion about your service provider but if you are happy with it, then stick with Breathe. If you have problems with your connection or you find that your email never gets through, then change to another ISP. It's up to you to decide if you are satisfied.

A connection speed of 115,200bps would be a very good rate if it were physically possible. This connection rate in your modem set-up is the maximum possible speed of the connection between your PC and the modem. 56kbps modems typically transfer data over the phone lines at around 46,000bps, although modems can achieve higher throughput of data using compression. You are probably getting good transfer rates if your ISP supports 56k connections – call it to find out.

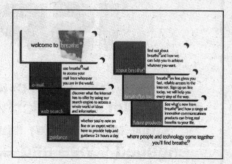

CATCH 22

I have recently connected up to the Internet with Global Internet. It took approximately four hours and a great deal of patience from the technical support staff to install the software. They talked me through all different procedures thinking that my modem was faulty because of the symptoms I described to them. To cut a long story short, it transpired that the problem was with the McAfee anti-virus program I had installed on my PC for safety before getting an Internet account.

I am reluctant to reinstall the program because I have been informed that some anti-virus programs of this nature can be more of a problem than an asset. This leaves me in a bit of a catch-22 situation – if I don't install the software, my computer is open to attack from any virus, if I do reinstall the software, I may experience difficulties with my Internet connection. Do you have any suggestions which may resolve my dilemma?

Anti-virus software can be a problem with some Internet software set-ups. I have never experienced problems myself, because I use an anti-virus program that is designed to work alongside Internet software without causing any of the problems you have had. I use Dr. Solomon's Home Guard software. It costs about £30 and is available from stores such as PC World, Dixons or any store that sells PC software. Visit the Dr. Solomon's home page at **http://www.drsolomon.com/index_new.cfm** for more information about the program.

JAVA JITTERS

Q

My present ISP, although possessing a Unix server, has it configured for lower-case file names only. I have started to use WebBurst to create Java applets, and when creating the applets it uses upper and lower case for the file names.

It is not possible to put everything into lower case, as it appears to screw up part of the code, and after a lot of emailing to the makers, I have been told to use an ISP which will allow both cases.

I use my Web site as a personal site, not a commercial one. I need an ISP which – in addition to the above – supplies CGI scripts and also has its server configured for Macromedia Shockwave. I have phoned several ISPs but they do not offer all of the above unless I pay for a commercial site. Do you know of any ISPs that have all of these facilities for a personal Web site?

A

The simplest solution would be to ask your ISP to allow upper and lower case file names which is a pretty standard set-up. But most major ISPs such as Demon Internet or UUNET Pipex offer support for upper and lower case file names and CGI scripting. As for Shockwave plug-ins for Web pages, all you have to do is upload the file to the Web server and embed the plug-in into your Web page. This will allow it to download just like an image file when it is called by the HTML code.

You can find out more about Demon Internet at **http://www.demon.net** and Pipex Dial at **http://www.dial.pipex.com**.

INTERNATIONAL ISPS

 Q How would I go about joining an ISP in Denmark. I will be moving over there shortly but I do not know which ISPs operate in Denmark at a local call charge.

A There are over 10,000 international service providers listed at The Directory at **http://www.thedirectory.org/**, including a list of Danish service providers. The Danish service provider list is at **http://www.thedirectory.org/for/acc/45.htm**.

FACE FAX

Q

I have a laptop that came bundled with Windows 95 and MSN. I tried MSN on a 30-day free trial and have just tried AOL on a 30-day trial. I prefer AOL, mainly because I can log on more successfully and more quickly. All the bundled software to send faxes, set up a modem, change Internet settings and so on is all based around MSN. If I want to use AOL, will I have to alter my Windows settings, uninstall files and purchase new software to send faxes and so on? I'd especially like to send faxes directly from Lotus WordPro, which I used to use a lot.

A

Sending faxes has nothing to do with your MSN or AOL settings at all. Any fax software you have should be completely independent of your Internet settings, no matter what service provider you use.

Once you have set up your bundled fax software to send and receive faxes, it's set up for good – no matter what else you do with your modem.

EXPLORING POSSIBILITIES

I have an account with AOL, and also a company account at work through our head office in Switzerland. The company account uses Internet Explorer 3. My problem is that while AOL and MSN work fine side-by-side on my company account, any other Internet account I install causes problems.

I want to add an ISP account to my work computer, but each one I have tried overwrites Internet Explorer. When I click on the company Internet icon, the PC tries to load up a new version of IE and connect through my new account. The IT department couldn't see a way round it, and just put everything back to normal after I deleted my ISP account. Why is it I can use AOL alongside my business Internet account, but not connect via a different service provider?

Would an ISP that uses Netscape Navigator solve the problem? Could you let me know which ones use Netscape Navigator, none of them seem to advertise that they use it.

You can only have one version of Internet Explorer active on your PC at any time. If you try to install more, the operating system gets severely confused. In fact, you only need one copy of Internet Explorer on your PC – you use the same version whether you connect using your company account or your private account.

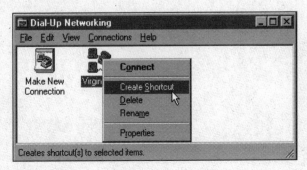

I guess that you are clicking on the service provider's or your own company's icon, which appear on the desktop when you try to connect to the Internet.

The trick is to click on the Dial-Up Networking connection for your company account or your service provider account, rather than the current desktop icons. This will ensure that you connect through the account you choose, rather than having the default account dial up automatically for you.

Go to the 'Start' button on the Taskbar and select 'Dial-Up Networking' from the Programs and Accessories pop-up menus. When the Dial-Up Networking window appears, the diallers for your service provider and your company account should be visible. There is just my Virgin Net dialler in the example on the previous page, but you get the idea.

Right-click on the company account dialler and select 'Create Shortcut' from the pop-up menu. Windows asks if you want to place the shortcut on the desktop, so select 'Yes.' Repeat this for your private account. Now, when you want to connect to the Internet, double-click on the icon of the dialler you want to connect with. After connecting to the Internet, you can select any Internet software you wish to use, including browsers, email programs or newsreaders.

If you are interested, the latest version of the Virgin Net software uses Netscape Navigator 3 as its default browser. Call Virgin Net on **0845 650 0000** for details.

AUTO RE-DIAL

Q I frequently get busy signals when I try to log on to my ISP. The technical support team says this isn't caused by a shortage of modems, rather it's a BT problem. Whatever the reason, I want Windows to keep trying to dial instead of making me do it. Is this possible?

A It's not only possible, it's simple. Automatic re-dial is a feature of Windows 95, but by default it's turned off. To turn it on, open the Dial-Up Networking folder in My Computer and from the Connections menu select 'Settings.'

Now click in the 'Redial' box to tick it and enter the number of retries and the period of time to wait between each.

TONE ON, TUNE IN

Q I installed my service provider's software and it seemed to go OK. But when I try to log on to my service provider, I get the message "No dial tone." I'm using a Pace 56 Voice modem which I know works because I tried it on a friend's PC. My service provider says it must be a modem problem, as I can hear the dial tone perfectly well and use the phone line to make and receive calls.

A It's fairly unusual for a working modem to report no dial tone on a working telephone line. In fact the only thing we can suggest is to go back to BT customer service (dial 150 – it's free) and explain that you want the line-gain tested. If the gain on the line is too low you might well be able to use it for ordinary voice calls but not with a modem. It's normally set to auto, but ask them to set it to three or four – much higher than this and it can start humming. BT will be reluctant to do this on the grounds that its contract only extends to supplying a voice line. Persevere – we're in the digital age.

BT Internet
What we offer
What others say
Payment options
What you need
Software provided
FAQs

CHAPTER 3

UNDERSTANDING MODEMS

Don't know what model your modem is? Stuck in the World Wide Wait when you should be surfing the Web? We can help

WHAT MODEM MAKE?

Q Is there any way I can find out the make and model of my internal modem? It was already installed inside my new computer when I bought it. The sales guys seem to have no idea at all about what's inside the PC, and were unable to help me. It is listed as an 'Internal Enhanced Modem' in the Modem control panel of Windows 95. I know that it is K56Flex, and that it's flash upgradeable to the new standards, but my problem is how to upgrade it without knowing who made it, and therefore, which site to visit.

A You can use one of the ATI Identifier codes in the Hayes modem command set to query your modem about its manufacturer. All modems respond to a set of commands sent by your PC. That's how it knows when to dial out or when to answer an incoming call. To send Hayes commands to your modem, you need to use a terminal emulator program. If you don't have a terminal emulator, go to the Tucows mirror site at **http://tucows.cableinet.net/term95.html** and download one of the programs there. I recommend either CRT or EasyTerm. Versions for Windows 3.11 are available.

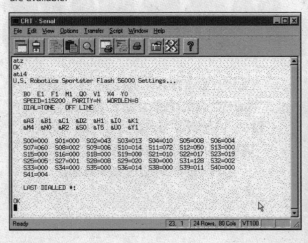

After installing the terminal emulator on your PC, run the program. Make sure that it is set up to detect your modem by checking the settings in the Options menu. You should set the terminal emulator to serial mode, RTS/CTS, 8, none, 1. You must specify the correct Com port for your modem, COM 1 or COM 2 – you can find this out by checking the modem's control panel.

After ensuring the settings are correct, type in 'AZT' in the main terminal window and press the 'Return' key. The program should then find your modem, and the modem should print 'OK' in the terminal window.

Now type in the letters A, T, and I followed by the number 4 – 'ATI4' – and press 'Return'. The modem should display its manufacturer and model number in the terminal window. Make a note of the modem's make and model for future reference. You should now be able to track down any ROM upgrades on the Web.

SLOW COACH

Q I'm coming to the end of my tether with a problem, so any advice you can provide will be gladly received. Last week I took delivery of a MESH Pentium II 233 PC with an internal K56Flex modem. According to the documentation it's a CommWave HSP 56K FLEX PNP modem. Everything works fine except the modem – it only ever connects to the Internet at 4,800bps. The result, as you can imagine, is an unusable, slow connection. I've tried connecting through three different service providers and the result is always the same. A friend of mine who is pretty knowledgeable about PCs has checked the modem settings and they all seem correct. He thinks that it's some sort of software problem – possibly to do with an initialisation string.

I've contacted my service provider, they tested the phone line and set-up and confirmed that everything looks okay. I've also contacted MESH who were less than helpful. They told me to reinstall the modem driver, but this had no effect. I've searched the Internet trying to find information from CommWave but they don't appear to be online. Do you have any suggestions that might remedy this problem? I'm very keen to get a decent connection so I can have a proper look at what the Internet has to offer.

A Internal modems can be a problem, especially because so many of them are manufactured by virtually unknown companies based in the Far East. It's almost impossible to get UK-based support from the actual modem manufacturer.

One question. Are you sure that you are only connecting at 4,800bps? Where is this figure coming from? If this figure is based on the information in the status bar at the bottom of your Web browser's window, then the connection is shown in kbps, not bps. This means that your connection is at 48,000bps which is actually slightly above average for a 56k modem.

But I have tracked down CommWave for you, it's based in Singapore. CommWave modems are made by a company called Multiwave, and you'll find its Web site at **http://www. multiwave.com/**. You can download new modem drivers from this Web site, and register online for technical support.

Make sure you read the instructions on the Web site, they are very specific. If installing the driver doesn't solve the problem, send an email to **support@multiwave.com.sg**.

ART OF NOISE

Q I have an internal modem, 14kbps and irritatingly slow. Hopefully, I'll get a 56kbps for my birthday. What gets on my nerves, or shall I say on my husband's nerves, is not the slowness – it's the noise it makes on connecting. I've read that there are ways to fix it. I've tried the volume on the modem thingy, but it does not work. What I've read is that there is another way of doing it, through an initialisation string. Could you please explain nice and slowly exactly how to do it?

A While the command to control the speaker setting in your modem is a simple Hayes AT command, actually getting it into your modem settings is a little more difficult. The command is 'ATLn,' where n is a number between 0 and 3.

ATL0 Lowest speaker volume
ATL1 Low speaker volume
ATL2 Medium speaker volume
ATL3 Highest speaker volume

To get the command into your modem, go to the 'Settings' command in the Start menu and select 'Control Panel.' Open the modem's control panel by double-clicking on it. In the Modem Properties box, make sure your modem is selected, and click on the 'Properties' button. When the Properties box opens, click the 'Connection' tab, then click on the 'Advanced' button at the bottom right of the box.

When the Advanced Connections Settings box appears, type ATL0 (or whatever you prefer) in the Extra Settings field. Then click on 'OK' to close each window in turn, and close the modem's control panel.

SNAILS PACE?

Q When setting up the Dialler Properties which connect me to my Internet provider, my modem – a new Pace 56 Voice Internal – is not listed as a choice in the Modem Type window. I have selected the Pace Microlin fx 32 Plus modem from the list, and I have selected the maximum speed as 115,200bps. I don't know whether this is the best selection to ensure I get the best possible Internet speed. None of the listed modems appear to be faster than 33,600bps.

A Windows 3.1 and 3.11 do not use modem drivers in the same way as Windows 95/98 and Windows NT 4.0 do. It's very likely that your PC will only be able to talk to your modem at a maximum speed of 19,200bps in any case. This is because of its hardware limitations.

But to maximise the potential of your modem, you should download the latest high speed COM driver for Windows 3.1/3.11 from the Pace Web site at **http://www.pacecom. co.uk/drivers.htm**. The file is called RHSICOMM.DRV and only takes a few seconds to download as an EXE file.

After installing the file on your PC, select the nearest modem in the list to your Pace 56 Voice Internal and keep the speed settings as they are. This should ensure the very best possible connection speeds for your Internet connections.

WHAT MAKE? (PART 2)

Q

I can't find out who the manufacturer of my modem is. Someone suggested I try typing in ATI4 into a terminal emulator, but there's still no joy. However, it does display the following string of numbers:

a007880284C6002F
bC60000000
r1005111151012004
r300011117000000
What does this mean?

A

I have tried the ATI4 method with some other modems. It works with some and provides the manufacturer's information, but with others it generates a string of numbers and characters similar to yours. Even a Hayes Accura 56K modem gives the same result. I suggest that you go to the Modems control panel and see how your modem is

described in the list. The name of the modem should be displayed in the window on the left. If it just says something like "56k

modem" then click on the Diagnostics tab and select the 'More Info' button. The modem information should be displayed in the window. Finally, if none of the above helps, contact the manufacturer of your PC. It should be able to provide you with the relevant information about your particular internal modem.

DRIVING ME MAD

Q I have a Gallant InterCom 56k PnP 56Flex Rockwell chipset modem. I have the inf Rev 1.4 driver which came with the modem. I want to know if there is any way I can get a more up-to-date driver because I can only seem to connect at around 33,600bps, and I think a newer driver will solve my problem. I have looked at the Gallant Web site, but it's not very helpful.

A I contacted technical support at Gallant Computer and they informed me that there are no updates available; the driver you have is the latest available.

It may be worth checking to see if your service provider supports K56Flex connections. It may have a different connection number to the one you are using.

The other thing to check is the maximum connection speed of your modem. Go to the Start button and select 'Settings,' then 'Control Panel.' Run the Modem control panel and click on the 'Properties' button. In the Maximum Speed box, select '115200' from the pop-up menu. Click on 'OK' to finish.

Gallant later contacted me, saying that the updates should have been available by the end of July, so it could be worth taking another look at the company's Web site, which you'll find at **http://www.gallantcom.com**.

CONNECTION TROUBLE

Q

I have a Hayes Accura K56Flex modem, but I'm having trouble connecting to my Internet service provider – Pipex Dial. Although I have followed all of the instructions on the Pipex Dial support pages, concerning setting up my connection using a K56Flex modem, it rarely manages to make a connection at all, and when it does, it takes a long time to negotiate the log-in sequence. I seem to have done everything right, so what am I doing wrong?

A

Because the K56Flex chipset from Rockwell has been around for a while, there are several different versions in various modems. Rockwell has three different levels of chip/firmware installed in its chips, and each of these different levels are incompatible with each other. So if your modem uses a version of firmware incompatible with the version used by your service provider, you will have trouble connecting.

Firmware is the name for software routines stored in read-only memory (ROM). The routines in the modem's firmware contain the K56Flex connection protocols. In most cases, firmware is fixed in ROM and cannot be changed without physically changing the

chips. In modems such as the Hayes Accura, the firmware is stored in a Flash ROM. This can have new versions of the software written to it by running an upgrade program on your PC.

The three levels of firmware can be split into these groups:

Versions v0.1 – v0.9

Versions v1.0 – v2.0

Version v2.0 and above.

Here are the characteristics of the three groups. Versions between v0.0 and v0.9 were beta code and rarely – if ever – worked. Versions v1.002 and v1.002b both work and are fully tested. Version v1.12 works on random occasions, but you may find that connection is lost after a period of time. Version v1.2 is the latest code and is generally regarded as the most stable. It works in all environments. Version v2.012 is transitional code which allows you to then upgrade your modem to V.90 compliancy. v2.012 is not compatible with any other version of the firmware.

If you have a Hayes modem, the optimum firmware is v1.10. Contact your service provider to find out which version of the firmware it supports. The version used by Pipex Dial is v1.161.

If your modem is flash upgradeable, you must obtain the correct upgrade file and download it into your modem. Note that you MUST use the correct upgrade code for your modem. DO NOT use a US code upgrade in a UK modem unless you have been specifically advised to do so by your modem supplier. To find out if there is an upgrade available for your modem, visit the UK Web page of your modem manufacturer. The Hayes site is at **http://www.hayes.co.uk**.

Note that modems running firmware revision 0.520 are not Flash upgradeable. If your modem is not Flash upgradeable, the only way to upgrade it to K56Flex is to return it for a hardware upgrade or replacement. You may be charged for this service.

BYTE THE BULLET

Q

I recently bought a 56k modem as an upgrade from a 33.6k modem, but I found that it was downloading really slowly, generally at 2.4k. I remembered a letter in *Practical Internet* that mentioned initialisation strings. I found one on the manufacturer's Web site and copied it. I wasn't quite sure what to do with it, so I pasted it into the Extra Settings box in the Advanced Connection Settings window, which seemed to solve the problem.

The only thing is that now, when I hold the pointer over the connection symbol in the bottom right-hand corner of the screen, it says 'Connected at 115,200bps,' which is obviously not true. What I am wondering is whether there is a program which shows the actual connection speed, because I want to be sure I've done the right thing by replacing my modem. It seems faster, but there's not a lot in it.

I realise 56k modems don't actually connect at 56k, but the further away from 33.6k (not to mention 2.4k) the better. Also, did I do the right thing with the initialisation string? More to the point, what the hell is an initialisation string anyway?

A

You must be careful when working out connection speeds. Remember that your Web browser displays the connection speed in kilobytes per second, while modem speeds are measured in kilobits per second. So when your browser tells you it is downloading at 2.4k per second, that works out as 2,400 x 8 = 19,200 bits per second or 19.2k. But this is still not the 46k you would expect from a 56k modem.

You have done the correct thing with the initialisation string by pasting it into the Advanced Connection Settings field in the

Modem control panel. An initialisation string is a series of codes that send instructions to the modem, ensuring that it is set up correctly. If your modem is now downloading faster, there is nothing else you need do. To get a true idea of the actual connection speed, you need a utility such as Net.Medic. You try this software for yourself, as it's on our cover CD-ROM. The program displays information about your connection including a real-time display of the current download speed, how long it takes to retrieve a Web page and the average download speed of the download. It's a very good utility, and I always run it when connecting to the Internet with my PC.

TONE UP

Q

I have a Pace Microlin 33.6 Fax'n'Data modem and I am perfectly happy with it. However, there is just one thing that is causing problems. When I have the fax program running in the background, it can not tell the difference between an incoming voice call and an incoming fax call. The poor voice caller gets an ear-hole full of fax squawk – it's happened to all of us at one time or another.

Can you tell me if there is any gadget, gizmo or software that can distinguish between incoming voice and fax stuff that will then route the call accordingly?

A

Your modem and fax software should already be able to automatically detect the fax CNG tones that are sent down the phone line by the transmitting fax machine while the phone is still ringing. Mine does this without any problem.

You need to check through the preferences of your particular fax software to make sure that you are not overlooking anything obvious such as CNG detection. One solution, although it is a rather unsatisfactory one, is to set up your fax software so that it answers after about 10 rings – this should give you ample time to answer the phone if somebody is at home.

The slightly more expensive option is a fax switching device called Fax Friend. This machine automatically detects fax and voice calls. You can get Fax Friend from electrical shops such as Dixons, Currys and PC World. The Fax Friend generally costs around the £50 mark.

JUST TOO FAR AWAY

Q

I've spent the best part of a week on the phone to ClaraNET and Motorola, trying to improve my connection speed from 26.4kbps. I use a Motorola VoiceSURFR 56kbps modem.

Motorola has said it's tried all its initialisation strings, and there is nothing more it can do. I've tried altering the data buffer settings, and tweaked the initialisation strings. In the end, Motorola says that I'm too far from my ISP. I'm in Wiltshire and ClaraNET is in London. As far as my ISP is concerned, it is able to connect using 56kbps technology. ClaraNET says the connection should be nearer 40kbps than 26kbps.

BT has adjusted the gain on my line, but it has made absolutely no difference. Do you think changing my ISP would help?

A

Unfortunately, 56kbps technology isn't as straightforward as getting a simple 56kbps connection. Your initial connection speed has little relation to download speeds when wandering around the Internet. Connection speed fluctuates between very low and very high speeds while online.

You should stick with ClaraNET – I don't think that you are 'too far away' from them. It shouldn't make any difference where your ISP is.

There's a little monitoring program you might find helpful – it's called Any Speed. You can download it from **http://www.kagi.com/yellow/default.html** to enable you to diagnose the health of your connection speed while you are logged on to the Internet.

MINOR OPERATION

Q

I have recently switched from a US Robotics 28.8kbps modem to a Motorola 56kbps Voice SURFR. When I initially set the modem up, it was working fine and continued to for several weeks. However, about four weeks ago a rather strange problem started.

When I try to connect to my ISP (Enterprise), or try to send a fax (via Microsoft Fax) the modem does not recognise the dialing tone. I know there is a dialing tone because I have plugged speakers into the modem, and I can hear it.

I have managed to get around part of the problem by changing the dial-up properties to 'don't wait for dial tone.' This works when connecting to my ISP, but has not solved the fax problem.

I have been informed that the local BT exchange has been updated to a digital type – could this have anything to do with it?

A

There is an outside chance that BT switching to a digital exchange is the cause of the ailment here. However, I think there may be some settings in your modem properties that need to be changed to rectify this.

Open the Control Panels window and double-click on the 'Modems' control panel. Then click once on the

'Dialing Properties' button at the bottom of the page. In the Dialing Properties window, make sure that 'Tone Dialing' is selected, that you have entered your local Dialing code and selected United Kingdom in the 'I am in:' box. The problem doesn't need a major operation.

BACK SEAT DRIVER

Q Because I couldn't get the correct software driver to connect my computer to my modem, I managed to get Windows 95 to detect the modem by itself. It decided that my modem is a 28.8kbps (28,800bps) modem even though it is actually a 33.6kbps device. However, when I connect to the Internet, a window on the monitor tells me I am connected at 57.6kbps. This can't be right, can it, as that's faster than the new 56kbps modems! I would be very grateful if you could tell me exactly what speed I am actually connected at, and could you please elaborate a little. Thanks in advance.

A Although the connection window tells you that you are connected at 57.6kbps, this is simply showing you the connection speed setting configured by Windows 95. In fact, your minimum connection speed will be 28.8kbps, but you should be connecting at the full 33.6kbps capability of your modem (provided your ISP supports this). When your modem connects to your service provider's modem, they 'talk' to each other and establish the fastest speed possible between them.

GET AWAY!

Q I have a 33.6kbps US Robotics modem, a UK model. I recently downloaded the x2 upgrade [for 56kbps access – Ed.] for my modem but was informed that the upgrade wouldn't work with my particular modem. Fair enough, I said, and contacted my PC vendor, Gateway 2000. Gateway told me my modem has x2 capabilities and already has the x2 upgrade on it. So I contacted my service provider and said I now had x2. I was given another access code to use which has 56kbps access.

What I want to know is, how do I turn the x2 feature on? Is it already on? Do I just need to dial my service provider? If so, then why does my Dial-Up Networking connection still state that I am connected at 33,600kbps?

A Provided your service provider supports the x2 protocol for fast Internet access, you shouldn't have to do anything – x2 just works. Unfortunately, you can't trust the speed estimate as reported by Dial-Up Networking, especially in the first release of Windows 95 where everything over 28.8kbps is reported as the COM port speed setting instead! To get a more accurate reading, why not try the evaluation version of Net.Medic, accessible from our cover CD.

Interestingly, if an x2 (or K56Flex) modem fails to negotiate a 56kbps protocol it falls back to V34, which is 33.6kbps. This can also happen if there's more than one analogue to digital step in the connection (another one besides your local modem connection). Ask your telephone company to check this. Try your modem on someone else's PC, preferably in a different town and with a different service provider. Whatever you do, on no account run a 'flash' upgrade intended for a different country on a 56kbps modem bought in the UK. Doing so won't break the modem, but it will ensure it never, ever, connects at 56kbps on this side of the pond.

COM AND GET IT

Q I have a cheap K56Flex modem and a service provider who supports this speed, but Windows 95 insists on installing my modem as a standard device. Can you tell me if there's any way I can make it work at 56kbps?

A Don't worry about it. The negotiation to establish a K56Flex connection is carried out between your modem and your service provider's kit, so it has absolutely nothing to do with Windows. Just make sure the COM port setting is 115,000bps to make sure it can always handle the data rate. If you find you aren't getting fast connections, then the problem is with the line or the modem, and not with Windows.

FAX OF LIFE

It turns out my modem can send faxes, but how do I make the fax part work in Windows 95?

Go to the Control Panel, select 'Add/Remove Programs' and click on the Windows Setup tab. You'll see Microsoft Fax as one of the options. If it isn't ticked, click in the box next to it and then click on 'OK.' Windows will ask for your 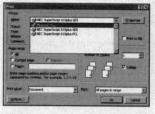 fax software installation disk, and then install it. Just follow the instructions onscreen. Afterward, you should find the fax

function on the list of printers in the Print dialog accessed from the File|Print menu option in applications. Select it and follow the instructions to send the current document or image as a fax.

PC PROBLEMS

Trying to fathom why a PC won't work takes time, which most of us don't have enough of. We can't claim to solve all your problems, but if it's to do with the Net, we'll have a go

MOTHER KNOWS BEST

Q I have a real problem trying to download large files and emails. I have tried all the usual suggestions such as connecting at off-peak times, using a different Web browser, trying a different modem configuration, using a Web cache and so on. I've even switched to a different service provider, but without success.

Here's an example. When downloading a 650K software upgrade from the local server which should take about five to 10 minutes to transfer, after 20 minutes only about 10 per cent of the file has downloaded. It seems that there is an initial transfer of data then everything falls asleep for minutes at a time.

I seem to have a good connection and I am using a 56k modem. I am new to the Internet so I am not sure if this is a common problem or not. Perhaps I am missing something fundamental. I hope you can help. I am using a 486DX2-66 PC with an external SupraExpress 56e K56Flex modem, running Windows 95.

A I think the last line holds the clue as to what is causing your problem. Unfortunately, it's probably your hardware – your PC. Because you are using a 486DX2-66 PC, it's very likely that the I/O hardware that drives the serial ports uses a chip called a 16550 UART. Now this chip can only transfer data at a maximum speed of 19,200 bps, effectively crippling your modem to a speed that's only a third faster than a 14.4kbps modem.

Your best bet, if you can't afford to buy a completely new PC, is to invest in a motherboard upgrade to a Pentium 133 or 166. On the other hand, a new Pentium CPU unit with 32Mb of RAM and a chunky hard drive can be found for around £500 in the large PC magazines like *PC Shopper* or *PC Plus*. You really should upgrade to a faster PC if you are going to be using the Internet.

WINDOWS 98 WORRIES

Q I'm not sure about switching to Windows 98 because I don't want to use a Web browser toolbar for my normal hard drive navigation. Everyone I know who has added the Windows Desktop Update to Windows 95 has removed it after a few days, the reason being that it's too confusing. My work colleagues and I would prefer to keep the interfaces for Web browsing and navigating the PC and network separate. Why has Microsoft imposed this crazy system on us?

A I'm afraid it's impossible for you to remove the Windows Desktop Update or Internet Explorer 4 from Windows 98 because they are now integral parts of the operating system. To be honest, the Windows Desktop Update isn't that bad – you don't get a 'Web browser toolbar' when you are browsing your hard drive, you get a hard drive toolbar.

Microsoft has developed a 'smart toolbar' system that detects what kind of window you are looking at and switches the toolbar automatically when you switch from a Web view to a standard folder window view. Microsoft has changed the look of the tools in the folder window toolbar, and added back and forward buttons, but all of the old tools such as cut, copy, paste and up one level are still there. They just look different. And you can always turn off the toolbar, and just keep the drop-down menus in exactly the same way as you could with Windows 95. Why did Microsoft impose the new interface on

us? To make things easier, so the Web, your hard drive and your local network can all be accessed and viewed in the same way.

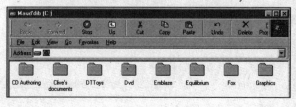

USEFUL UPGRADE?

Q

I'm thinking of upgrading to Windows 98, but I don't want to use Internet Explorer 4 because I'm not very keen on the Windows Desktop Update it installs. I'd rather stick with Internet Explorer 3.

A

If you upgrade to Windows 98, you have no choice in the matter of the Windows Desktop Update and using Internet Explorer 4. Both of these features are integrated tightly into the system, so much so that the listing for Microsoft Internet Explorer 4 no longer appears in the Add/Remove Programs control panel. This

means that you cannot remove the IE 4 features or the Windows Desktop Update. You can customise the Windows Desktop Update so that you get the traditional view of drive and folder windows and so on, but the navigation toolbars at the top of each folder window are now the same as the toolbar in IE 4. I was very wary of the Windows Desktop Update when added to Windows 95 because it slowed down the operating system so much, but it works seamlessly in

Windows 98, and you soon get used to the new way of navigating around Windows. If you must use Internet Explorer 3 for your Web browsing, then you'll have to stick with Windows

95. But it's important to note that Internet Explorer 4 is much more compatible with technologies such as Dynamic HTML, Java and JavaScript than Internet Explorer 3 can ever be.

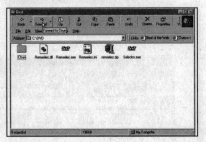

DOWNLOAD DIFFICULTY

Q I have recently tried downloading software from the Internet but I cannot open or run any of the files. According to the book Easy Web Publishing with HTML 3.2, I should install the software by selecting 'Run' from the Start menu and enter the file details and follow the steps for installation. This did not work because the file could not be found.

Clicking on the files with the right mouse button and then selecting the Open command results in the error message "The C:\WINDOWS\
DESKTOP\xxxxx.zip file is not a Windows Help file, or the file is corrupted."

I'm having the same problem with Install Shield Extractor EXE files when these appear instead. Again, the files were corrupted.

Can you could tell me the correct installation procedure for installing files downloaded from the Internet? At the moment I have deleted all of the items as they appear to be corrupted.

A I don't think there is anything wrong with the files you have downloaded at all. I think you're having a problem using Windows 95 itself. Follow these steps to download files and run them.

First, set up a Downloads folder on your C drive or on the Windows 95 desktop. To create a folder on the desktop, hold down the right mouse button and choose the 'New Folder' command. This is where you will store the files. On a Web page, right-click on the file you want to download and select the 'Save Target As...' command. This lets you choose the destination folder using the file selector.

Once the file is downloaded, there are two simple ways to run it. Say the file is called INSTALL.EXE, and it's in the Downloads folder on drive C. Go to the Start button on the Taskbar and select 'Run.' When the Run box appears, click on the 'Browse' button and use the file selector to go to the Downloads folder on drive C. Select the 'INSTALL.EXE' file then click on 'Open.' Now you're back at the Run box, click the 'OK' button and the program will run. Alternatively, open the

Downloads folder and double-click on the file using the left
mouse button – this also runs the program.

2486 DO YOU APPRECIATE?

I've been given a 486DX PC by my company (it was being thrown out after an upgrade) which I plan to use for Internet access at home. It has Windows 3.1 on it. Would I be able to install an internal modem?

The short answer is yes. However, I assume the PC has two working serial ports already, so an external modem is a simpler option. If you still want to install an internal modem, there are some things you need to know. Windows 3.1 likes a continuous run of serial port numbers or it can get confused. This means either disabling your existing COM2 and making the modem COM2 instead – the best solution. You do this in the BIOS or via a jumper on the motherboard or I/O card (depending on the exact set up of your PC – check the system manuals, if there are any).

Alternatively, you can set the modem to COM3, but this shares an IRQ with COM1, so you'd have to put the mouse on COM2 to stop them interfering with each other. COM1 could always then be used for something else when you're not using the modem.

You also need an internal modem you can set to a specific COM port, such as the Diamond SupraExpress 56. Most internal modems are now plug-and-play, which isn't too useful with Windows 3.1. It's generally a lot less fuss to fit an external modem to a Windows 3.1 system.

BROKEN WINDOW

Q Windows 95 crashes a lot while I'm online. I use the original version that came with my computer when I bought it, but I've been told that there's a bug fix for Internet users with my version of Windows 95. Is this so?

A Yes, you'll find it at **http://www.microsoft.com/windows/ software/krnlupd.html**.
What it actually fixes is the Internet TCP/IP driver (the basic software for setting up a Net connection) which originally had a memory leak. This means Windows uses up all its memory while you're online, and then falls over. Unfortunate, really. This is a self installing file, so just download it and run it. It may fix your problem completely, or it might just reduce it. This all depends on exactly why it's happening. Not everyone will benefit to the same extent.

POWER TO THE PC

Q I'm thinking of buying a new PC to get more out of the Net, but I am confused about one thing. Can you tell me if there any relationship between the speed of a PC's processor and the speed with which I'll be able to get stuff off the Web?

A No, but so bald an answer needs qualifying. Web download speeds are so slow – considered as a data input stream the PC has to cope with – that the PC can cope with it without too much hassle. However, some Net activities do benefit from a faster machine. A speedy processor will help you run multimedia elements on certain Web pages, such as Java or ActiveX applets (once they've downloaded). Faster chips make it easier to explore Internet telephony and videoconferencing as well, and lots of memory (RAM) helps too. The limiting factor on Web download speeds to the home or office is the speed of the connection between you and your Internet service provider. Currently, the fastest dial-up speed available is 64Kbits per second, but this is only possible for most people via ISDN (Integrated Services Digital Network). Unfortunately, an ISDN service is expensive.

RETURN OF THE MAC

Q **Is it better to buy a Mac or a PC to get on to the Internet?**

A Mac lovers will doubtless burn my effigy, but I would go for a PC. The reasons? A modern PC, bought mail-order, will cost less for more features, have more up-to-date software available at lower prices and cost a lot less (in terms of money and hassle) to upgrade. From personal experience, getting parts for older Macs can also be a headache – by old, I'm talking a 1995 machine –

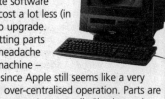

since Apple still seems like a very over-centralised operation. Parts are expensive, as well. Check out the cost and availability of Net-ready Macs, and you'll see a significant price difference between PCs. That said, if you've just bought a Mac and you're happy with it, fine, as these days, they're easy to get on the Net and many service providers now offer specialist Mac support.

THE WORLD WIDE WEB

Having general problems with the Web? No need to panic. This is the section where we sort out all the common queries about the Net

THE BIG FREEZE

I have tried to upgrade to version 4.05 of Netscape Navigator for Windows 3.1, but after installing it onto my PC, whenever I run it, it makes my PC completely freeze up. I have uninstalled it and reverted to v3.01 which works fine.

You haven't given me much information about your system, but I would hazard a guess that you may not have enough memory installed in your PC to run Netscape Navigator 4.05. You really need 16Mb of RAM to run the latest version of Navigator 4 under Windows 3.1.

COOKIE MONSTER

How much personal information does my PC give away when I visit Web sites and how can I control what info is given to whom and when? What is a cookie? I am using a Compaq 4640, Windows 95 and Internet Explorer 4.

Your PC will only pass on the information contained within the Preferences (in Netscape Navigator/Communicator) or in the Internet Options in Outlook Express (in Internet Explorer 4). So the most that can be passed on is going to be your name and email address. You can control this information by entering false details into your preferences, but this means you won't be able to send email messages while using the false settings. Briefly, cookies store information about you in your temporary Internet files folder. When you return to a Web site that has sent you a cookie, you are recognised and messages, or content specific to you, can be generated by the Web site. A good example is the Microsoft Network. When you return to members-only pages on MSN, you don't have to enter your username or password because it's entered automatically for you.

CUT IT OUT

Q Although I am finding using the World Wide Web fun, I'm getting a bit fed up with the continual cut-offs. Almost every time I connect to the Web, I'll be happily moving from page to page and then everything just gets stuck for no reason. It happens on whatever page I visit – it doesn't matter which Web site I am looking at – nothing moves at all. Then, after a couple of minutes of nothing happening, my browser just cuts the connection.

I use Internet Explorer 4 and NetDirect for access to the Web. I can't help but find the whole thing a bit suspect, though. I know things get busy, and I do connect at the busy times, but every time after getting cut off, I immediately reconnect and I can get straight through to the page I was trying to look at.

Tell me, is it possible for an under-resourced service provider to time you out at busy times, just to give an impression of availability by keeping their customers moving instead of giving an engaged tone? If not, what is going on? Also, is it possible to stop my browser from automatically terminating the connection?

A It's highly unlikely that your service provider is cutting you off from the Internet after a specific length of time. If a service provider started doing that, it would quickly lose its customers.

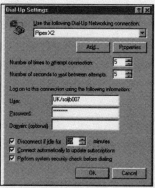

It's more likely that Internet Explorer 4 is freezing up, rather than your ISP shutting down your connection. Your best option is to uninstall Internet Explorer 4 using the Add/Remove Programs control panel and reinstall it from your NetDirect CD. You can specify how long your connection remains active using the Internet control panel. Go to the Start button and select

'Settings,' 'Control Panel.' Double-click on the 'Internet' control panel to open it, and then click on the 'Connection' setting. Click on the 'Settings' button, found in the Connection box, and then enter a suitable setting in the 'Disconnect if idle for…' section. When you've done all this, click on 'OK' to finish.

SONIC BOOM WEB

Ever since I installed the Web accelerator NetSonic, I have had a problem accessing Web pages that I have previously visited when I am in Offline mode. I have checked, and the pages are within their expiry dates on my hard drive. Even though I have now disabled NetSonic, I am still having the same problem.

I have tried emptying both the NetSonic cache and the temporary Internet files, and trying again with the same result: no access in Offline mode. The History file within Internet Explorer 4 shows the files to be available – there is no 'barred hand' adjacent to the Web pages – but on selecting a Web page, nothing happens.

If I choose to access the temporary Internet files via the Internet Options within IE 4 and attempt to open the Web pages from there, I come up with the alert 'Running a program on this item might be unsafe.'

I have contacted Web 3000, the publishers of NetSonic, and Microsoft in an attempt to resolve the problem. Web 3000 admits that it knows about the problem but at the moment it has no solution. Microsoft just suggested that I reinstall Internet Explorer 4, but this made no difference.

Because of the nature of NetSonic, and the way it works, it disables access to the Temporary Internet Files folder because it uses its own cache. To view pages when offline using Internet Explorer 4, you can disconnect from the Internet, but DO NOT switch to Offline mode.

Instead, leave the browser in Online mode and browse through the history file as you normally would. The pages should now be displayed, but they load from the NetSonic cache, instead of the Temporary Internet Files folder. This will solve your problems.

COME BACK IE 3!

Q I have an old 486 running Windows 95 with limited hard drive space. I am browsing using a partial version of Internet Explorer 3 supplied by CompuServe; the email features are missing. I would like to know if it is still possible to obtain the full version of IE 3 anywhere so I can experiment with different service providers – everyone seems to supply IE 4 these days.

A Internet Explorer 3.02 is available for download from the Microsoft Web site. The address is **http://www. microsoft.com/ie/download/** – but you'll find that IE 3 doesn't actually include any email software. IE 4 is supplied with a separate email and newsgroup program called Outlook Express. You can use Internet Explorer 3.02 alongside a freeware email program such as Eudora Light from **http://www.eudora.com**. This should satisfy all your browsing and mail needs.

As a final note, the latest version of Internet Explorer 3.02 has been updated to be fully year 2000 compliant, so if you are using IE 3, then you should update it as soon as possible.

COMPATIBILITY PROBLEMS

Q

I have Internet Explorer 3.02, and it works fine, and I had no troubles in installing it. But, when I got a free version of Internet Explorer 4.0, I could not install it on my computer. I know it is a problem with the computer, because it works perfectly on my older P75 machine. I have also tried installing from other CDs and I have the same problem.

Here's what happens. It begins to install, and part way through the installation it skips to 36% installed. Then it displays an error message that says "Setup failed. Please try quitting all other programs, and then try again." I have tried again several times, but I always end up with the same problem.

A

The only thing I can think of is that you may have an early version of Windows 95 which is not fully compatible with Internet Explorer 4. There have been many reports of problems installing IE 4 on machines with versions 4.00.950 and 4.00.950 A of Windows 95. You should have no problems installing IE 4 on PCs with versions 4.00.950 B and 4.00.950 C of Windows 95. To find out which version of Windows 95 you have, go to the Start menu and select 'Settings,' then 'Control Panel.' Double-click on the 'System' control panel and select the 'General' tab in the System Properties window.

The first item is the System information. If it says you have

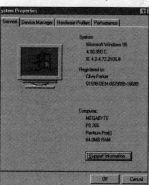

Microsoft Windows 95 4.00.950 or Microsoft Windows 95 4.00.950 A then you may have problems installing IE 4. If you have the B or C versions, then you should contact your PC supplier's technical support line. The contact details should be available when you click on the 'Support Information' button at the bottom of the System Properties window.

GIF CONVERSION

Q

I have a problem which I hope you can help me out with. The first problem is to do with Internet Explorer 4 and GIF files. I recently upgraded from Internet Explorer 3 to Internet Explorer 4 when I took out an annual subscription to Direct Net Access. Previously, I had been testing AOL and had downloaded a number of GIFs. After upgrading to Internet Explorer 4, I could not view these GIFs any more but I can view newly saved GIFs saved using Internet Explorer 4.

I recently discovered that these unreadable GIFs can still be viewed using IE 3 on a separate PC. Is there any way of converting these GIFs to IE 4 acceptability, or loading IE 3 as another version of Internet Explorer on the same machine? I have the same problems viewing using Paint Shop Pro and other image viewers.

A

The only thing I can think of is that images you had downloaded using AOL were in some way encoded or encrypted or just plain corrupted. I must admit I can download GIF files using AOL without any problems, so it looks as though some corrupting influence has been at work on your hard drive.

Now, if a GIF is viewable in IE 3 it should also be viewable in IE 4. It's a standard file type viewed using the same routines in both browsers. Try viewing the images in IE 3 and right-clicking on the images, then using the 'Save Image As...' command to save the images using different file names.

And if you can view the files in IE 3, there's absolutely no feasible reason why you can't view the files in your graphics software such as Paint Shop Pro.

Finally, you cannot have versions of Internet Explorer 3 and Internet Explorer 4 on the same PC – you must decide between one or the other.

CRASH TEST DUMMY

Q

My problem is with Internet Explorer 4. Having used Internet Explorer 3 at my old job, I very much enjoyed the simplicity of its History function and the ability to delete single entries from the History list. With Internet Explorer 4, I seem only to be able to clear the entire History and I cannot delete individual entries which I no longer want to see. Worse than that, whenever I open the History it causes Internet Explorer 4 to crash – as you can imagine, in Windows NT 4.0 this is an unusual occurrence! Can you help me?

A

Internet Explorer 4 should not cause Windows NT 4.0 to crash under any circumstances. There may have been a problem with the installation so it might be a good idea to completely uninstall Internet Explorer 4 and then re-install it.

After re-installing, open the Internet control panel and select the 'Advanced' tab. In the browsing section, make sure that the 'Browse in a new process' box is ticked: this makes the browser more stable by assigning it with a separate block of memory.

You can remove single items from the history list in Internet Explorer 4. Open the History list by clicking on the 'History' icon, then open a folder containing items you want to delete. Select an item by right-clicking on it, causing a pop-up menu to appear.

Select the 'Delete' option and the single entry is deleted, leaving the rest of the History list untouched. Repeat the process as required.

ON TARGET

Q

I like to download movie files and I have recently done something stupid and I cannot back-track. When I chose to download a movie I was always given the choice of opening the file or saving it to disk. The default always came up as 'Save To Disk' and because this is what I wanted to do, and it was the default position, I opted for ticking the 'Don't Show Me This Again' box. The problem is it now opens the file and I want to bring back the option to save or open but can't find how to.

A

To save a file to disk instead of viewing it in Internet Explorer, right-click on the link and select the 'Save Target As...' command in the pop-up menu. When the file starts to download, the file selector box opens asking where you would like to save the file.

TWICE AS NICE

Q When using Internet Explorer 4, I want to close the browser and automatically disconnect. I've searched through all of the various options, settings and so on in IE 4's network connections, modems et cetera, but without any luck. I know that I can set up Outlook 98 to automatically disconnect after sending and receiving email, so why hasn't Microsoft included an option to automatically disconnect when IE 4 is closed?

Why click twice when once will do? When I close my browser I want to disconnect. On more than one occasion, having suddenly thought of something, I've quickly closed the browser and jumped up from my seat to go and follow that thought, only to find an hour later that there's a nice little message asking me if I want to disconnect. Is there anyway to disconnect automatically after closing the browser?

A I don't think you've thoroughly checked all the options. Like yourself, I sometimes wander off and leave my PC connected to the Internet.

Go to the Internet control panel and click on the 'Connection' tab. In the Dialling section, tick the 'Disconnect if idle for...' box and enter the number of minutes to wait before disconnecting. Click the 'OK' button and it's done. But what's wrong with disconnecting manually? After all, you only have to double-click on the connection icon in the Windows 95 Taskbar. Surely that's not too time consuming, is it?

CACHE FOR QUESTIONS

Q

What is the precise function of the cache? I have accumulated hundreds of them on my hard drive. They seem to fill up with a lot of GIF and HTM and JPG files. In order to release space on the hard drive, can these files be safely deleted without affecting any of my programs?

I also seem to have accumulated a lot of 'cookies.' What are these and are they useful, necessary, or just a nuisance? Can I safely delete them? Is there a way I can prevent them from attaching themselves to my computer?

A

You can safely empty out your cache files. Your browser uses the cache directories to store images and pages to speed up viewing time. If a page on the Web has changed since your last visit, it's downloaded over the Internet. If it hasn't changed, it's loaded from the cache, saving download times. Even individual images on Web pages are cached in this way.

In Internet Explorer 3, use the 'Options' command in the View menu (or select the 'Internet' control panel from, er, Control Panels). Select the 'Advanced' tab in Options then click on the

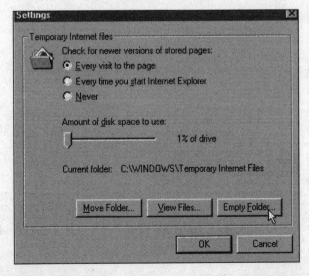

'Settings' button in the Temporary Internet Files box. In the Settings box you can set the amount of drive space to be used as cache, view the files or empty the cache by clicking on the 'Empty Folder' button. The procedure is similar in Internet Explorer 4 and in Netscape Navigator. See the picture opposite to find out how to clear the cache in Internet Explorer 3.

Cookies are text files that store information about you on your hard drive. When you visit a site that uses passwords or is for members only, your browser automatically sends the details to the Web site saving you the task of logging in. Cookies are also used for the personalisation of Web sites. A site could read your details from the cookie it has set up on your hard drive, and greet you with a "Welcome Rupina, it has been seven days since your last visit," message. A Web page can only react to a cookie that it has placed on your hard drive; it cannot access cookies left by other pages.

If you don't want to receive cookies, both Internet Explorer and Netscape Navigator have options in their security preferences that allow you to switch cookies on and off. Some people regard them as a security risk, but I have never had any problems with them. Cookies are always enabled in my PC and Macintosh browsers.

LOST SCREENSAVER

Q

Every time I try to download a screensaver – or anything else from the Internet – Internet Explorer 4.0 always seems to open up WordPad and then close it down again. At first I thought this was because it was trying to view a 'readme' file, but when I go to the display control panel there is no sign of the screensaver. Can you please help me – I have downloaded several screensavers and other free software packages from the Internet, but I cannot seem to find them after they have downloaded.

A

I am not sure why WordPad would open when you download a file, and it is not something I have been able to duplicate on my PC. Anyway, here is the procedure to follow if you want to make sure you are downloading files correctly. Using Windows Explorer, create a new folder on your C drive called 'Downloads.' This is where your downloaded files from the Internet will be stored.

When you connect to a Web page which includes files and software you want to download, click on the file. Instead of using the right mouse button, use the left one. This makes a pop-up menu appear under the mouse cursor. Choose the 'Save Target As…' command from the menu and wait for the file selection box to appear. Use the file selection box to choose your new Downloads folder as the folder to save the file into, and then click on the 'OK' button. The file will now download to your PC.

After you have disconnected from the Internet, use Windows Explorer to view the contents of your Downloads folder. The file you have downloaded to your PC should now be in the Downloads folder; simply double-click on the file to run it. This

will then run the setup program and install the software on your PC. That should end the pain.

UPDATE ME

Q I was installing Internet Explorer 4 when I was confronted by a question that completely baffled me. The installation Wizard asked me if I wanted to install a Windows Desktop Update which will give me a Web-enhanced active desktop. What is this, and is it something I should install?

A The update basically adds new features to Windows 95, enabling you to view HTML files on the desktop, and updates the system so that each drive or directory window can act as a mini-version of Internet Explore. This gives you an HTML view of your operating system. I have found that it slows the system down dramatically on a P166 PC and can be quite frustrating to use. And, if you have only just got used to Windows 95, it can be very confusing to have yet another way of accessing information on your PC. One final thing. It has been reported that the update causes some earlier versions of Windows 95 to crash. There are two release versions of Windows 95, release A and release B. To find out which release you have, go to the System control panel and study the information about your version of Windows.

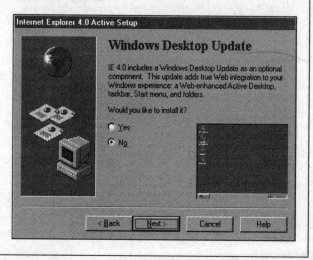

MESSENGER IN A BOTTLE

Q I'm thinking of upgrading to Netscape Navigator 4 as my main browser, but I've been put off slightly by a piece about Navigator 4 printed in a rival Internet magazine. A reader who asked about sending and receiving email with Navigator 4 was told that the previous version of the browser must be used for email. Surely this can't be right. Please let me know what the situation is with Netscape Navigator 4 and email support.

A Although the email element of Netscape Navigator 4 is now classed as a separate entity from the browser, you can still download various elements of the Netscape Communicator suite individually. That means you can add Netscape Messenger or Messenger Express to your Netscape Navigator setup. For more information visit the page at **http://home.netscape.com/comprod/products/communicator/messenger.html**.

Alternatively, you can download Netscape Communicator 4.5, which contains lots of useful extra features. It's a big download for the full version, but well worth it. It's also on our cover CD most months.

VIRGIN NAVIGATOR

Q

Are there any UK service providers that let you log in fully using Netscape Navigator 4.0? I want to use Netscape Communicator 4.5 for access to the Web, to pick up my email and to use the new Netcaster feature.

A

Virgin Net supplies Netscape Navigator as its standard Web browser, and there's no reason why you can't download Communicator 4.5 and use it instead of Navigator.

In fact, there's absolutely nothing to stop you from using Netscape Communicator even if you use a service provider that supplies you with Internet Explorer 3 or 4. You can easily stop

Internet Explorer from being the default browser using the Internet control panel. To do this, open the Internet control panel and select the 'Programs' tab. At the bottom of the screen is a checkbox that asks you if you want to make Internet Explorer the default browser. Clear the box to stop Internet Explorer from launching when you connect to the Internet.

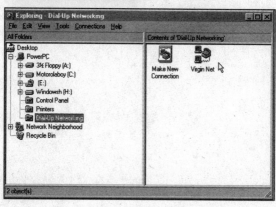

When you install a service provider's software onto your PC, it creates a dialler in the Dial-Up Networking folder.

You can connect to the Internet by double-clicking on the connection icon for your service provider instead of running Internet Explorer to connect.

Go to the Start button and select 'Programs,' then 'Windows Explorer' from the pop-up menu. When Windows Explorer opens, select the 'Dial-Up Networking' folder in the directory tree on the left and then double-click on the connection icon in the right hand window.

After you have connected to the Internet, you can then run Netscape Communicator and do as you please.

ZIP ME UP

I was wondering if I can use my parallel-port model Zip drive for something while I am online. Most of the time, the drive just sits on top of my tower case doing nothing in particular. Can I use a Zip disk as the cache folder for Netscape Navigator as I wander around on the Internet? Would it slow things down if Netscape is accessing the Zip drive, instead of using my hard drive? If it is okay, it will allow me to have a 100Mb cache without using up lovely hard drive space.

You can select any drive you like to act as your cache directory, although 100Mb seems to be rather a large cache size. I manage quite happily on my PC with a cache of just 8Mb. I'm not sure what the access speed of a parallel-port Zip drive is (I use the SCSI version), but if you can happily run Windows software from the Zip drive, then it should be okay to use a Zip disk as a cache disk. Just remember to have the correct disk in the drive when you run Netscape Navigator.

EXE MARKS THE SPOT

Q I have recently downloaded the following components of IE 4 from Microsoft's Web site – the Internet Explorer 4.01 upgrade, Outlook Express, the FrontPage Express upgrade and multi-language support. I want to know how I can back up these downloaded files in case I need to re-install Windows 95 in the future. If I have to re-install Windows 95, I don't want to download all of the IE 4 files again.

Also, how can I change the directory where Outlook Express stores the newsgroup messages. At the moment, the directory setting on my system is C:\mswin95\Application Data\Microsoft\Outlook Express\News\. I want to store them on my other hard drive. Is this possible?

A To save downloading the updated components again, the best thing you can do is to keep the EXE installation files from the Microsoft Web site. After installing the components, store the installation files in a directory on your spare hard drive, instead of deleting them. Then, if you have to install Windows 95 again, you already have the IE 4.01 upgrade and all the bits you need.

As for your Outlook Express problem, I've spent around an hour searching through every possible option in Outlook Express, but I can't find out how to change the default directory settings.

COMPLICATED ADDRESS

Q My browser will find a site if I just type in the middle part of the address (the part with the company or organisation name), so what's the point of the all the other parts? Why is it that complete Web addresses are so long and complicated?

A Good question. The Web address of a page is known as its URL, which stands for Universal Resource Locator. This defines the address of the object or resource you're accessing, as well as the means (or protocol) used to access it. http is the protocol used to communicate with Web servers, ftp is used to access file servers, mailto accesses mail servers and so on. However, as most people access Web servers most of the time, the http can be assumed. But not always. For example, **nic.funet.fi** is a Finnish site with ftp and Web capability. If you want the Web, you can type it in as it is, while to get ftp you have to use the full URL of **ftp://nic.funet.fi**. On the other hand, most ftp servers are called ftp, so browsers assume that if you type in something such as ftp.microsoft.com you actually want **ftp://ftp.microsoft.com**. If you don't understand these kinds of distinctions, then you may never find the sites you actually want. URLs are important. As for the other part, a Web server address must have two parts: a domain name and a server name. Consider Digital (a computer and software company) which has a company domain of digital.com. It also has a Web server called www at digital.com, so the full address for it is **http://www.digital.com**.

This is the most common type of Web address, and if you type in digital this is where your browser will go, but Digital also has at least one other publicly accessible Web server, called altavista. If you type in **altavista.digital.com** you'll end up at the famous Web search engine, but not if you rely on your browser to fill it in for you. This kind of problem crops up repeatedly because people assume a Web server must be called www – not so.

PORN FREE

Q

My whole family uses my PC for Web surfing at various times, but some of the material I'm interested in isn't suitable for my children. Does any of this material remain in the PC after I disconnect and turn it off?

A

Yes, it does if you're still using your Web browser's default set-up. To speed Web page display, your browser assumes you will want to go to the same page again, so it keeps each page it downloads in a cache on your hard drive for a while (until it fills up the cache and has to start deleting older files to make room for new ones). If you view a page, click on a link and then click on the Back button, your browser reloads the page from the local cache rather than downloading it again from the Net.

Normally, it only does this for pages downloaded in the current session (since you last logged on). However, it doesn't clear the cache at the end of a session.

To do this in Internet Explorer, go to View/Internet Options. On the General tab you'll find a Delete button for Temporary Internet Files. Click it to clear the cache. You can also reduce the cache to zero bytes to effectively turn it off. The process is much the same in Navigator (via Edit/Preferences). Out of interest, you can also clear the History list at the same time, which, while it doesn't save pages, does contain a list of the addresses of the last 20 or so sites you've visited for easy reference.

OPENING FAVORITE

Q I know I can make a Web page on my hard drive appear as my opening page when I start my Web browser. Is it possible to turn my Internet Explorer Favorites list into my default opening page? Most of the places I want to go are there, so I think it makes sense to make this my starting point.

A The Favorites list is actually a Web page called bookmarks.htm in Netscape Navigator, so find bookmark.htm (in Program Files within the Navigator folder) by browsing for it in Navigator, and just set it to be your default opening page as you would with any other.

In Internet Explorer, the Favorites folder really is a folder, not a page, so it works a little differently. Where it is depends on how your system is set up. If you happen to be the only user of a standalone PC, it's simply the Favourites folder in the Windows folder.

However, while making it the default page for Internet Explorer 4 is simple – just type in the full path to your Favorites folder – the effects aren't what you might expect. What happens is that IE4 opens as a standard folder window and then, when you click on a link, a new Internet Explorer style window opens to show the Web page.

In some ways this is neater than having the Favorites Explorer bar open down the left side of the browser window as it doesn't take up any display space.

DRAG AND DROP

Q   **I know I can save Web pages to my desktop, but is there a way to put a link to a Web page on the desktop?**

A   Just drag a link straight to the desktop and drop it. You can do this from a Web page or any other document with a live link. You can then drop the link into other documents such as email, and send them to people. Actually, each link is a tiny text file. You can make your own using Notepad. Open it and type:

    [InternetShortcut]

    followed on the next line by:

    URL=http://www.yoursite.com

    where the URL is a real Web address. Simple really.

    Out of interest, you can also open your Favourites list as an ordinary folder and treat the links in it in the same way. Start Internet Explorer, select the Favourites and hold down the Shift key while clicking on 'Organise Favourites.' You then get a standard folder window with the Internet shortcuts inside.

SPEED COUNTS

Q

There appear to be several programs available claiming to speed up downloads from the Internet by anything up to six times. Do these actually work?

A

You're presumably referring to commercial software such as PeakJet and Net Accelerator. What these programs do is to find all the 'links' on the page you've just downloaded and start downloading from those links in the background. If you sit and read the page for long enough, and then click another link on it, the utility will already have downloaded the link and the content should appear straight away. It sounds an excellent idea, but in practice these programs don't work that well unless you're on a fast, permanent connection to the Net (which most readers won't be). On dial-up connections they don't do enough to make a difference. For example, these programs don't differentiate between links on ad banners and those which are crucial to the Web site. Also, if you're checking out a list of locations provided by a 'search engine,' the links you want to be downloaded are on the page you've just come from, not the one you're reading.

The other major problem with this approach is that it doesn't take into account the way most people browse the Web. If you check a page, follow a link to another one, then to another one and so on, little of the work done in the background is going to be of any use to you – only if you constantly retrace your steps does it help. The efficient way to work with the Web is to open several windows at once and have each following a line of enquiry. This way, you're making the most of your Net connection to download material you actually want to see – not random links you probably have no intention of following. Our advice is to save your money and concentrate on changing your Web browsing habits to maximise your connection.

LANGUAGE BARRIER

Q

Occasionally, a Web site I'm interested in turns out to be in a foreign language – and I don't speak any. I realise it isn't practical for Web authors to create multiple different language versions but it seems to leave us with a problem. Is there an easy way around this?

A

The simplest solution is to copy the Web address of the page. Open your Web browser and go to **http://www.babelfish. altavista.digital.com**. Paste the Web address into the box provided and click the translate button so the text is translated into English. This Web site works brilliantly, with one exception: if the Web page author has used graphics for text information, these parts don't get translated (because they're pictures, and not text).

INDIE KID

 Q Is there much in the way of original, independent music on the Net? I'm told that there's lots, but wouldn't it take an awful long time to download digitised music using a modem?

A There's lot of original indie music online, some there legally, but a lot in breach of copyright. What makes it practical is the MP3 codec. A codec is an implementation of a compression/decompression algorithm and MP3 stands for MPEG Level 3. So now you know. MP3 can produce near CD-quality sound from digitised audio files compressed at ratios as high as 14:1. This effectively means a 1Mb download provides about one minute of CD quality music, so a three or four minute song can be downloaded in 15 to 20 minutes using only a modem. At weekends, we're talking 20p

per song. MP3 has unleashed a tidal wave of home-grown and garage music on the Web. Check out **http://www.4treasures. com/jermidi/music.htm** for more info, a discussion of MP3 and links to sites. The standard MP3 player is WinAmp, available from **http://winamp.lh.net/main.html**, as well as a number of other sites. However, Microsoft's NetShow supports an even more efficient version of the MP3 codec so you can use it instead – if it doesn't come as part of the Internet Explorer Web browser, get it from **http://www.microsoft.com**.

IE4 UPGRADE FAILURE

Q After upgrading my early copy of Internet Explorer 4 with a later version from a magazine cover disc, my PC is behaving rather strangely and crashing far more than it used to. Should I re-install the earlier version even though some of the features weren't working on it?

A No. First uninstall all versions of Internet Explorer from your PC using Add/Remove Programs in the Control Panel. Then re-install the latest version of Internet Explorer 4. While you're at it, we suggest not installing the Active Desktop unless you like living dangerously (not to mention slowing your system fairly dramatically). The main problem, if you're interested, is incompatible Virtual Java Machines in the various versions of Internet Explorer 4, which don't appear to be upgraded along with the program itself. Uninstalling Internet Explorer 4 and all associated features (and Internet Explorer 3 afterward) seems to clear it all out. You should find it then works okay. If your PC has 16Mb or less, consider upgrading it. With Internet Explorer 4, Windows 95 really needs more RAM memory.

ALL ABOUT EMAIL

Email is a wonderful, cheap and easy way of communicating with friends and business contacts. To try it is to love it!

EMAIL CONFUSION

If you get a free email address from – as in my case – Hotmail, why would you want to download Eudora Light? Surely the Web-based email service would be all you need. Or am I missing something?

Nope, rest assured that you're not missing anything obvious – you don't need a dedicated email program such as Eudora Light if you are using a Web-based email service such as Hotmail. Web-based email uses completely different protocols than stand-alone email clients, so the mail cannot be viewed by Eudora. However, you can use Eudora Light to read your email if you hold an email account with a service provider.

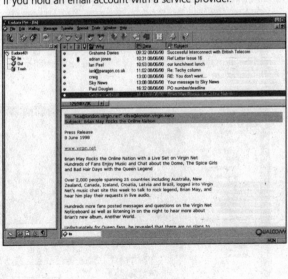

FILES NOT FILED

Q

Can you please help me get my outgoing email to appear in the sent mail file of Netscape Navigator 2? Everything was fine until about six months ago when Windows 95 went all pear-shaped on me and I had to use the recovery disc to get it going again. Since then, all of my outgoing messages have not been recorded in the sent mail file although the email is being sent OK. I hope that you can help me out.

A

Netscape Navigator 2? That's getting a little long in the tooth now, ask Virgin Net to send you a CD with the latest version of its software. If my memory serves me correctly, there should be an option in the Mail and News preferences where you can choose where your sent emails are stored. If the box is not ticked, then your mail is not saved even though it is sent. Check through the preferences of Netscape Navigator 2 until you find the correct option. It may also be a good idea for you to reinstall your Virgin Net software.

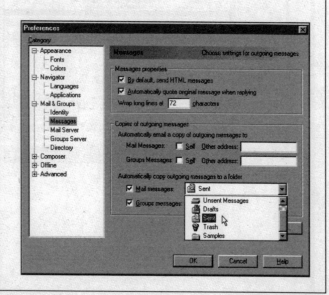

GET YOURSELF CONNECTED

Q I would like to know if there is a way to receive an email without going on the Internet, and have it show up on my desktop or as an icon of some kind? Any information would help. I have tried my service provider, but it really wasn't much help.

A I'm afraid not. You must connect to the Internet to receive email – how else could it get onto your computer? It's one of the basic fundamentals of the Internet: to receive information from it you must connect to it. You need to read up a little on how the Internet works: Try our sister magazine, *Internet Access Made Easy* or one of the many Internet books on the market. There are so many titles available it can be confusing, but I recommend Using The Internet, published by QUE. Some beginner's books can be too simple and a little childish and patronising in tone, but this book manages to strike a good balance. The fourth edition is now on sale from all good book stores such as Dillons or Waterstones, and costs £27.49. If you want to order it, quote the ISBN number 0-7897-1584-8.

MY EMAIL WON'T POP

Q

I use CompuServe as my service provider and I have recently converted my email service to POP3 email and I now use Microsoft Outlook 98 as my email software. I also have a Yahoo! Web-based email address. I want to retrieve my Yahoo! email using Outlook 98, but when I try to set it up, I am not able to do so, and I get the following bizarre error message: 'The settings you specified are incorrect, The server is behind a firewall. (Refer to the system administrator), The server is temporarily down.' Can you tell me if there is there a way of circumventing this?

A

This kind of question is turning up at an increasing rate – you are one of many readers who have asked a similar question about accessing Yahoo! email services using POP3 this month. Most Web-based email services can only be accessed by visiting the Web site where the service is available. This means that you can only read and reply to email while connected to the Internet, thus running up your phone bill. This is true of Hotmail, Netscape Mail, AltaVista mail and many of the growing band of Web-based services. Yahoo! Mail now has a POP3 option if you have signed up for a Yahoo! Online account (**http://online.yahoo.com**), enabling you to use email programs such as Outlook 98, Eudora or Outlook Express to access your Yahoo! mailbox. But this option is only available if you sign up and pay $14.95 a month – around £10 – in the same way as you would pay for any other service provider. So you can still access Yahoo! Mail for free over the Web, but you won't be able to access it though your POP3 email software unless you pay for an account.

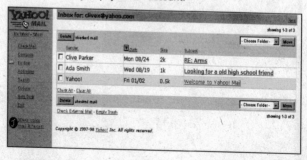

THE **BIG BOOK** OF
INTERNET ANSWERS

LONDON CALLING

Q If I email someone in another country, does it actually work out cheaper than phoning them, or would it cost the same as an international call?

To this end, if it is cheaper to email, how do I set up a personal chatline? Would I first have to set up a Web page? Also, some of the techie talk in your magazines has me a little baffled. What do the abbreviations HTML and URL stand for?

A Sending an email to someone in Los Angeles is a lot cheaper than making a phone call to the same person because you are only making a local call to your service provider, not an international phone call.

It's not really feasible to set up a personal chatline on your Web pages if they are hosted by your service provider. But you can actually have pretty good conversations with people using email as your messenger service. Remember that most email reaches its destination in under 15 minutes anywhere in the world. I regularly 'chat' with people all over the world in this way, sometimes exchanging a dozen or more emails over the course of a day.

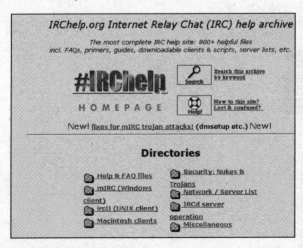

IRChelp.org Internet Relay Chat (IRC) help archive

The most complete IRC help site: 800+ helpful files incl. FAQs, primers, guides, downloadable clients & scripts, server lists, etc.

#IRChelp

Search this archive by keyword

HOMEPAGE

New to this site? Lost & confused?

New! fixes for mIRC trojan attacks! (dmsetup etc.) New!

Directories

- Help & FAQ files
- mIRC (Windows client)
- ircII (UNIX client)
- Macintosh clients
- Security: Nukes & Trojans
- Network / Server List
- IRCd server operation
- Miscellaneous

If you want to chat to a friend in 'real-time,' where you can see each other's comments being typed in, you need to get yourself onto Internet Relay Chat (IRC). An IRC channel, maintained by an IRC server, transmits the text typed by each user using the channel to all of the other users using the same channel. Most IRC channels are dedicated to specific topics, usually reflected in the name of the channel. If you and your contact both agree on times to use IRC, then you can chat in real-time for the price of a local call. But it's easy to build up large phone bills by using IRC for hours at a time. For more information on IRC, visit the IRC Help Homepage at **http://www.irchelp.org**. The address of the IRC Help Homepage is called a URL: it stands for Uniform Resource Locator. The code used to create Web pages is called HTML: this stands for HyperText Markup Language.

NET BENEFIT

Q

My service provider is Global Internet and I am using Internet Explorer 4 with Outlook Express. I have used email successfully on many occasions, but I just cannot send email to a colleague. He works at an NHS hospital and uses a non-Internet address. Are there different formats for email and can Outlook Express be used with these formats?

A

Your colleague probably uses the NHSnet system if he is based at a hospital. Using NHSnet it is possible to send email internally on the system between hospitals, but it is also possible to send and receive mail externally to normal Internet email addresses. You should be able to send email to your colleague using Outlook Express without any problems. You just need to know the correct way to enter the email address.

The easiest solution is to get your friend to send you an email. Their return address will be included in his message in the correct format. When you receive the message from your friend, open the Inbox of Outlook Express as usual and double-click on the message to open it in a new window. Go to the Tools menu and select the 'Add to Address Book' command, then select 'Sender' in the sub-menu. All the details are added to the address book, and the actual email address is displayed in the 'Email Addresses' window. Click on the 'OK' button to update the address book. When you want to send a message you can select the address from the Address Book.

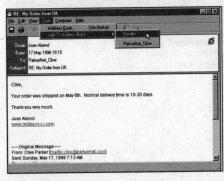

CLEAN UP OPERATION

My Net niggle is with Outlook Express. I have used the Tools/Options/Advanced/Clean Up Now command to clear out unwanted newsgroup information from the newsgroups I no longer subscribe to. However, even though the messages have been successfully deleted, a list remains of the newsgroups I previously subscribed to with the option to restore. I do not want this option and would like to clear the list. How do I do this?

The Clean Up Now option you have described only clears the messages from your cache folder; it does not unsubscribe you from the newsgroup itself. Using this option still leaves the newsgroups in the list of subscribed groups. To unsubscribe from a newsgroup in Outlook Express, right-click on the group and select the 'Unsubscribe' command from the pop-up menu. The newsgroup now disappears from the list. For good.

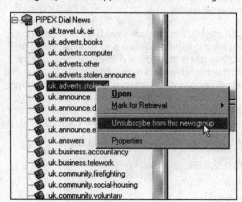

CONTROL FREAK

Q I would like to use Outlook Express to control my email but am having problems finding some details. I require the following information:

Incoming Mail (POP3) server.
Outgoing Mail (STMP) server.
I have already looked at the help on Yahoo! Mail but it doesn't provide this information.

A You won't find the information you need to run your Yahoo! Mail account using Outlook Express because Yahoo! mail doesn't work in the same way. It's a Web-based application and it does not use POP3 and SMTP servers in the same way as email access provided by a service provider.

If you want to set up Outlook Express with your service provider's mail servers, you must contact your service provider's technical support line. They will provide you with the correct details you need.

READ THIS AND WEEP

When I am online using Internet Explorer 4 and hit the 'Read Mail' button, Outlook Express boots up. This is fine until I do a Send and Receive. When I do this, Outlook Express tries to connect me to my ISP again but gives me an error message telling me that the port is already open. Surely it is possible to send and receive mail while logged on to Net using IE 4, isn't it?

You shouldn't be getting this problem. Outlook Express should detect that the connection is already open. It's worth checking out the setting. Go to the Tools menu and select the 'Options' command. Select the 'Dial-Up' tab, then make sure that the 'Automatically dial when checking for new messages' is unchecked with no tick in the box. This should stop Outlook Express from trying to dial when you are already connected.

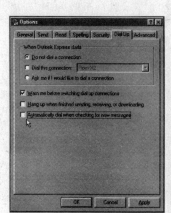

VIRUS HOAX

Q

I am writing to warn readers about an email virus I have received a warning about. Here is the text of the email:

"If you receive an email titled 'WIN A HOLIDAY' DO NOT open it, as it will erase everything on your hard drive. Forward this letter out to as many people as you can. This is a new, very malicious virus and not many people know about it. This information was announced yesterday morning from Microsoft, please share it with everyone that might access the Internet. Once again, pass this along to EVERYONE in your address book so that this may be stopped. Also, do not open or even look at any mail that says 'RETURNED OR UNABLE TO DELIVER' as this virus will attach itself to your computer components and render them useless. Immediately delete any mail items that say this. AOL has said that this is a very dangerous virus and that there is NO remedy for it at this time. Please practice cautionary measures and forward this message to all your online friends."

What should I do if I receive a message like this?

A

You will not receive any mail containing the WIN A HOLIDAY heading because it's a hoax. It's very similar to the so-called 'Good news' email virus hoax that was going around the Internet a few years ago.

In fact, even if a program containing a virus was attached to an email, there's no way that the virus can be activated by simply reading the email. Any executable program attached to an email has to be run manually by the person receiving the mail for it to have any effect on your system. The US Department of Energy has a specialist team that deals with computer viruses and hacking. It is called the CIAC (Computer Incident Advisory Capability). Here is what they say on the subject of email attachments:

"For a virus to spread, it must be executed. Reading a mail message does not execute the mail message. Viruses have been found as executable attachments to mail messages, but they must be extracted and executed to do any harm. CIAC still affirms that reading email or using typical mail agents, can not activate malicious code delivered in or with an email message."

So, simply reading an email CAN NOT install or activate a virus on a PC or Mac.

For more information about hoax viruses, see the Urban Legends page at **http://urbanlegends.miningco.com/library/weekly /aa030798.htm**.

E PLEASE BOB

 At the moment I only require email access. Do you know if there is a company who will provide email only?

NetDirect Internet provides a cheap and easy to set up email-only service. The account costs £17.59 incl. VAT per quarter, or £58.75 incl. VAT for the entire year – there is also a £11.75 set-up fee. You can contact NetDirect on **0181 293 7000**.

MISSION IMPOSSIBLE?

Q How do you work out what someone's email address is? In *Mission: Impossible*, Tom Cruise appeared to make up an email address, and the message sent reached the correct person. Is it really as easy as this to find an address? Where can I find the email software used in the film?

A You can't actually work out an email address just by typing in a made-up name. It may seem perfectly logical in *Mission: Impossible*, but it bears no relation to the way real email works.

In the vast majority of cases, the main part of the email name is supplied by the service provider. If, for instance, you have an AOL account, your email address will end in **@aol.com**. But if you have a PIPEX Dial account, then your email address will finish with **@dial.pipex.com**. Web-based email addresses end in the same way.

The first part of an email address is usually set by the user of the account, and is generally something to do with his or her name. If I had an AOL account, my email address might well be something like **clivep@aol.com**, **clive.parker@aol.com** or perhaps **cp@aol.com**. It really depends on the individual's particular choice.

If you work for a big company with its own Internet domain name, then the last part of the address reflects the company name. Examples are **netscape.com** and **microsoft.com**. Again, individual names make up the first part of the email address.

It's impossible – no pun intended – to dream up an email address that works as Ethan Hawke's does in *Mission: Impossible*. And the software doesn't exist either, it's just pretend. In fact, I've thought about it hard, and I've never actually seen the Internet or email accurately portrayed in a film to date. Has it ever been portrayed correctly?

MAIL SCAN

Q

I'm mailing from a Web site design firm, and a few of our clients have asked us if we can configure their Microsoft Office Outlook application to use Internet Mail to periodically scan for new email from their server or ISP.

We have been going over the program to see how this works. One thing the program asks for is server information – Outgoing Email (SMTP) and Incoming Mail (POP3). The idea won't work without this info, but will ISPs be willing to give away this information? If not, how do we get around this?

A

This information can be obtained routinely from your service provider's help desk. Or, if the ISP uses Netscape Navigator or Internet Explorer as its email program, the settings can be found in the Preferences or Options section for mail servers. In other words, it's not a major problem.

This information is also found in the Preferences of practically every email application, so it should be easy enough for your

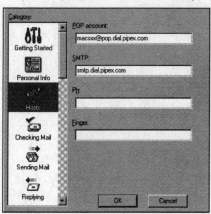

clients to take a look at their settings to find the information. It's pretty easy to find the server names. Here are the settings for my copy of Eudora Pro and Netscape Navigator.

CONFUSED@WALLY.NET

What do the different parts of an email address actually mean? It's very confusing.

As already mentioned, email addresses are split into two parts, before and after the @ sign, pronounced 'at.' The part before the @ sign is referred to as the mailbox. This can be a name of a person or a department within a business, such as **support@wallynet.com**. The part after the @ symbol is the domain and is usually made up of the name of the service provider followed by **.com**, **.net** or **.org**, or it could be followed by a country code such as **support@wallynet.co.uk**. There are many different domain suffixes.

EMAIL ON THE MOVE

Q I'm using Outlook Express as my email program on my laptop, so I can get mail while I'm on the move. The only problem is that once I've downloaded my email onto the laptop, the messages are deleted from the mail server. This means that I can't download them onto my desktop PC when I get back home. I use Eudora on my home PC, and this lets me leave mail on the server. Is there any way to do this in Outlook Express?

A You can set up Outlook Express to leave mail on the server for collection by another PC (or Macintosh) later. Go to the 'Tools' menu of Outlook Express and select the 'Accounts' command. Select the account you want to modify – in this example it's the ParkerNet account – then click on the 'Properties' button. In the Account Properties window, click on the 'Advanced' tab. The third section down – called Delivery – lets you choose whether you want to leave mail on the server, and even allows you to specify how long before it's deleted. Click on the 'OK' button to finish.

HIDDEN IDENTITY

Q

I write seeking advice in relation to email and multiple email addresses. I use BT Internet as my service provider, and I believe my account allows me to have up to five different email addresses. My current email address is rather obvious and personal. I would like to use this service to create a less personal email address for use when I am not among friends. An obvious instance would be the gaming and chat zones, where one might want to conceal one's true identity.

I currently use Internet Mail as my default email program and have access to Eudora Light, neither of which support multiple email addresses. I would therefore appreciate your advice on what readily-available software supports multiple addresses, and whether you have any recommendations or preferences. Hope you can help with this query.

A

You may be surprised to hear this, but I would recommend Microsoft's Outlook Express here. It's an easy-to-install and easy-to-use email program, which also supports multiple addresses. On top of that, you can use it to access newsgroups. Outlook Express is available as part of Internet Explorer 4, and you can download it from the Microsoft Web site at **http://www.microsoft. com/ie/** or install it from one of the many cover CDs available with PC magazines. I believe that the next version of the BT Internet software will include IE 4 as the default.

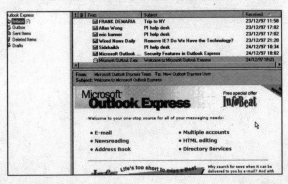

SPAM ATTACK

Q I have an account with AOL and I keep getting mass emails. Is there any way of stopping them?

A Mass mailings of junk email – sometimes known as 'spam' – is a big problem for AOL subscribers. AOL has a system of filters set up to help you cut out all of the junk mail you are getting. You can set up the filters in the Member Services area of AOL quite easily. The filters can be used to block all email, all email except that sent by AOL members or you can set them up to block messages from specific email addresses. Much of the junk mail comes from a few well-known addresses, so it's quite easy to block. If you have any problems, you can contact AOL member services on **0800 376 5432**.

ATTACHED TO HIS MAC

Q I have a friend who has a Mac and he is trying to send me attachment files of pictures from a Kodak Photo CD. I have an email account with Netcom. I have spoken to Netcom's technical support, and although the company has tried hard to give me a few solutions, none of the ideas has worked as yet. The files are attached as "mac/binhex 40" files. I've tried to use WinZip to open the files, and it keeps telling me that I don't have a viewer capable of seeing this image.

I'll try to send you the complete email message if you need it. The things that I see in the WinZip program are just characters such as 2?!!5^((b and so on.

A The files your friend is sending you from his Macintosh are in BinHex format, a file encoding system on the Mac similar to the UUEncode system commonly used by PC systems.

There are a couple of solutions to your problem. If you both use Eudora Light or Eudora Pro as your email software, attachments sent from a Mac can be decoded and read by Eudora on your PC. In fact, Eudora lets you choose between BinHex and UUEncode for attachments, so your friend could send the files UUEncoded rather than BinHexed. You can get Eudora Light for the Mac and for Windows from **http://www. eudora.com/**.

The other solution is to get StuffIt Expander from Aladdin Systems. StuffIt Expander decodes many encoded and compressed file types for the Mac and for Windows including SIT, ZIP, ARJ, ARC, GZ, UUE and HQX formats. You can download StuffIt Expander from the Aladdin SystemsWeb site at **http://www.aladdinsys.com/**.

CALIFORNIA DREAMING

I have a friend who has recently moved to California and I would like to send him pictures and images. What is the best way of doing this? I would be very grateful for any information on this topic.

You can attach image files to email messages using either of the major browsers or any up-to-date email application, e.g. Pegasus Mail or Eudora. Mail programs allow you to attach a file in one of the menus, or on an icon in the toolbar. Select the 'Attach' option, then use the file selector to choose the file you want to send to your friend.

EMAIL MELTDOWN

Q

My email stopped working last week, which turned out to be extremely inconvenient. When I phoned technical support I was told it was down for maintenance and upgrades and would be up again the following morning. Do all Internet service providers behave in such a cavalier fashion, just turning off services when they feel like it?

A

Running an ISP is a complex business, and servers are complex pieces of computer hardware. Things can, and do, go wrong. However, while most ISPs are now extremely reliable, servers must sometimes be taken offline for maintenance and upgrades. This is known as 'scheduled downtime' and is always pre-announced.

You'll find your ISP maintains a page or pages at its main Web site with information on scheduled maintenance tasks, known problems it's working to fix, software upgrades, phone number changes, new modem protocols supported, and other important information. You should get into the habit of checking these pages at least once a week to avoid getting caught out. This is just good preventive practice, similar to checking oil, water and tyre pressures on your car.

WAITER! WAITER!

Q I use ClaraNET, and keep having problems with Outlook Express, which says it cannot find the host. The ClaraNET helpline say that all my settings are OK and that it's a bug in Outlook Express. Have you any ideas ?

A Outlook Express does have bugs, and you can find a comprehensive list of them on the Web at **http://www. okinfoweb.com/moe/bugs/**.

Microsoft also has a support page for Outlook Express (with less emphasis on the bugs, though). However, your particular problem hasn't been reported. Just to see if you really have got all your host settings correct, install Eudora Light from our cover CD-ROM. If Eudora doesn't work either, then the problem is almost certainly caused by the settings at one end or the other. If it does work, you appear to have found another bug in Outlook Express.

Eric Miller's User Tips for:

Microsoft **Outlook Express**

[Back] [Home] [Next]

Bugs List

Search OE User Tips	Attachment Icon, but No Attachment
Board of Editors	Can't Stop IE Dialer
Bugs List	Character Limit in Mailto Links
Builds History	Character Set Problems
Connectivity	Compacting Errors
Digital IDs & Encryption	Data Migration in Business Cards
Features Requested	DID Security Level Cannot Be Changed
General	Downloading Messages Already Marked as Read
Guest Articles	Email Addresses Not Resolved
Mail Client	Encryption and DID Data Not Saved
Message Formatting	Errant Offline Termination Notice
News Reader	Hanging Up Non-OE Connections
Windows Address Book	Hard Carriage Returns
Reference Links	Hotlink Message Size Limit
Webmaster	Importing Changes Message Date
	Inbox Assertant Issues
	Indenting Automatically Works in Both Directions

WHICH ADDRESS?

Q

There seem to be several different kinds of email addresses on offer from different service providers, as far as I can see. While most now offer multiple email addresses, they seem to work in different ways. Can you explain the differences and tell me which is best?

A

Alright, but first we need to look at domain names or the answer won't make sense. Domains are the part after the @ sign in an email address. Let's say you were with the fictional service provider, Betanet. Its domain might be **betanet.com**, so your email addresses at Betanet would normally be **tom@betabet.com**, where tom is your user name on the system. However, if the service assigns you a meaningless name, as with UUNET, you can usually set up an email alias to make it friendlier. So, you may be assigned the name **abc123@betanet.com**, but then set up an alias for it called **tom@betanet.com**. Now, any email to either of these addresses will find its way to you. Please note there's only one real email account there. However, many service providers, including UUNET and AOL, enable you to set up multiple email

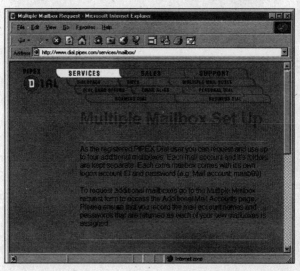

addresses on one dial-up account, each with its own password. So you could also set up: **dick@betanet.com** and **harry@betanet.com**. A few service providers actually allow you to have multiple dial-up accounts on one registration; one for each email address. This usually means you have access to more than one dial-up account (which could be at separate locations). It's unusual, but UK Online, for example, operates this way. Each will have the form: **tom@ukonline.co.uk**.

Finally, there's the virtual email account. Let's say betanet.com creates an address for you in the form: **aname@tom.betanet.com**. What's actually happened here is that Betanet has set up a local domain for you. Any name in front of the @ sign will still be an email to Tom's account. A number of service providers operate their email like this including Direct Net @ccess. The best solution depends on what you want. Unless you need email accounts with separate passwords, virtual email addresses provide unlimited email names for any purpose and you can have your email software filter them into different folders when they arrive. If different people will be using your machine for email, go for the multiple email account solution.

SHOULD I UPGRADE?

I've just found out that there's a more recent version of my email software. So I checked around and discovered more recent versions of much of my PC software available on the Internet. Should I upgrade or can I continue to use the versions supplied by my service provider?

Presumably you're running Windows 95, so check to see if your software is 32-bit or 16-bit. This info should appear in the About panel under Help or in the documentation. If it's 16-bit, then it's worth upgrading to a 32-bit version as these work more reliably with Windows 95. However, if you're already running 32-bit versions and you're happy with them, fine. It's always worth checking the blurb associated with new software; it may have a bug fix or a useful new feature.

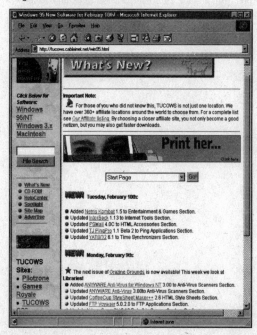

USING USENET

Newsgroups are an excellent way of chatting with people who share the same interests as you. Make sure you don't miss out on all that fun...

BUDDY FAN

A friend of mine mentioned the newsgroup alt.fan.buddy-holly. I am unable to locate this newsgroup on either my BT news server or on DejaNews. Can you tell me how to get there?

Of course. All you have to do to find the newsgroup is point your Web browser at **http://wren.supernews.com/** and then type **alt.fan.buddy-holly** into the search box. You will then be taken to the newsgroup.

KEEP ME POSTED

Q Is it possible to post messages to newsgroups using email? Also how can I find out which Web sites my kids have been surfing while I've been out? Finally, how can I play music/sounds in the background while surfing the Web?

A Technically you can't email to a newsgroup, only to an individual email address. Newsgroups use a different Net protocol. However, many programs combine newsgroup and email functions, such as Microsoft's Outlook Express (part of Internet Explorer 4). Staying on the subject of IE 4, if you are running this program, simply click the 'History' icon on the toolbar to see what sites your kids have been visiting during the past 20 days (by default, but you can lengthen this period via Internet Options under the View menu). If you use Netscape Navigator 4, hitting 'CTRL H' will bring up a similar History function. Alternatively, one of the Net filtering programs such as CyberPatrol (on our CD-ROM) will log every site visited in a somewhat more secure manner (your kids can delete History links in IE 4). The simplest way to hear music while you surf the Web is to put the radio on, or stick an audio CD in your CD-ROM drive. Or sing...

FILTER TIPS

Q

I use Internet News in Internet Explorer to read and reply to newsgroups, but find a great deal of unwanted material in each newsgroup as well as a huge amount of cross posting. How can I make sure I only get the postings I want?

A

This problem can be so bad in some newsgroups that it's hard to tell what the topic is without knowing the newsgroup name. One reasonable approach is to subscribe to a set of newsgroups but access it twice per session. The first time, you only download the subject headers. Mark the postings you think will prove interesting and then log on a second time to download the postings you've selected. It's slightly more hassle, but saves a lot of time overall. Alternatively, if you're willing to settle for less accuracy in exchange for less effort, try a newsreader with a filter feature. This enables you to specify all sorts of criteria for downloading postings and attachments. You'll find lots at: **http://www.winfiles.com/apps/98/news.html**.

An impressive example is Grabber, which enables you to set up unlimited filters using a variety of criteria.

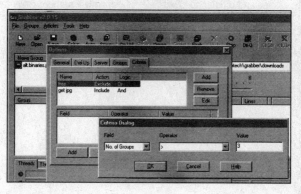

NO NEWS IS BAD NEWS

Q I can get a free email address from Hotmail [http://www.hotmail.com – Ed.] and even free Web space, but where do I find a free news server for newsgroups?

A Providing newsgroup access is a much bigger drain on the resources of a service provider than email or Web space. The problem is the sheer amount of news postings (more than half a gigabyte per day) and the way people use it – usually with automatic downloads from subscribed newsgroups. As a result, news servers work hard and, if made public, tend to become unusably busy. That said, there are always a few publicly accessible news servers around – but access tends not to last. Through self preservation, the providers restrict access to those coming in via their own modems or leased lines. However, it's fairly easy to automate searches for publicly accessible news servers, and there are a number of sites on the Net maintaining lists of those they find. Try **http://www.thenet.co.uk/~ dobbin/pubnews.html**.

By the time the list is published most are inaccessible, so you must expect to try several before you manage to get a working one and to change news servers frequently – perhaps every few days. The few service providers and other organisations which provide permanent free access tend to carry only specialist newsgroups, and most definitely do not carry the hugely popular alt.sex groups.

SMASHING TIME

Q

I am interested in subscribing to the newsgroups about my favourite band, the Smashing Pumpkins. Can I access the newsgroups using an email package?

A

Newsgroups ('Usenet') are regarded as the last bastion of the original, text-based Internet which was established in 1969. Usenet is a huge number of discussion groups (around 30,000 at the last count) each devoted to a specific subject. Messages sent, or 'posted,' to each group can be read by anyone in the world who subscribes to that particular group.

The easiest way to read newsgroups is to use your Web browser – Netscape Navigator 3, Netscape Communicator 4 or Outlook Express (part of Internet Explorer). Each of these have built-in newsreading components which let you read the contents of any newsgroup available from your service provider. Note that not all service providers supply access to all of the groups. In general, UK-based service providers will supply to all of the English-language newsgroups. Some newsgroups that the service provider deems unsuitable may not be available, usually those with explicit sexual content.

Name	Unread	Total
Local Mail		
news.dial.pipex.com		
alt.binaries.startrek	49	49
alt.binaries.starwars	24	24
alt.binaries.ufo.files	3	3
alt.binaries.warez	50	50
alt.binaries.x-files	20	20
alt.binaries.warez.ibm-pc	810	810
alt.binaries.pictures.joanne-guest	40	40
alt.binaries.satellite-tv	10	10
alt.binaries.screen-savers	74	74
alt.binaries.sounds.mp3	4019	4019
alt.startrek	567	567
alt.startrek.borg	36	36
alt.startrek.creative	407	407
rec.arts.startrek.reviews	20	20
rec.arts.startrek.current	1386	1386

LOYAL SUBSCRIBER

Q I have read that that my ISP offers around about 20,000 newsgroups. Is there any way I can set things up so I only view the groups that interest me?

A Because there are so many newsgroups, it's common practice to 'subscribe' to newsgroups you are interested in. Here is how to subscribe using Netscape Communicator's Collabra newsreader: Run Netscape Communicator and select the Collabra Discussion Groups command in the

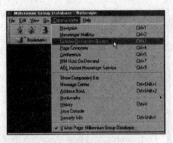

Communicator menu. When the Netscape Message Center window opens, select the Subscribe to Discussion Groups command in the File menu. The subscription window opens and the full list of groups is downloaded from your service provider. Because there are so many groups, it's best to use the Search for a Group utility. Click on the 'Search for a Group' tab and type a search word in the Search for: line. Then, click the 'Search Now' button. A list of every newsgroup containing your search word appears. To subscribe to a group, click on the dot in the Subscribe column so it changes into a tick. You can search for as many other words as you like. Click on the OK button when you've

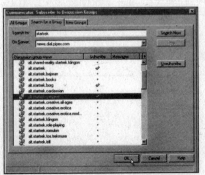

finished. When you look at the Message Center, a list of all the subscribed newsgroups appears, along with the number of messages in each group. To read the messages in a group, double-click on its name.

UP IN FLAMES

Q I play skittles down at my local boozer. After a good match I love nothing better than being able to discuss my chosen sport with people all over the world in the newgroups. But is there any way I can stop receiving flame messages and spam?

A Some newsgroups are gatherings of the more fanatical Internet users in the world; bigoted and opinionated in the extreme. If you upset someone by saying the wrong thing, using your right to free speech, you could end up receiving a stream of abusive email explaining exactly why you are wrong and they are right. Or it could just be abusive for the sake of it. This practice is called flaming. An easy way to extinguish flame email is to alter the settings of your newsreader program, whether it's Outlook Express, Netscape Communicator or FreeAgent, so you have a false name and email address. If you are anonymous, you won't get the fallout. This will also prevent you from being spammed by companies that compile marketing lists from the newsgroups.

I'M UK, YOU'RE UK

Q

Can you give me a list of any UK-based newgroups? How should I go about tracking them down?

A

Usenet can appear very US-dominated, but don't forget that there are a couple of hundred UK-based newsgroups as diverse as **uk.food+drink.archives**, **uk.media.tv.friends** or **uk.rec.pets.misc**. Scroll down the list of newsgroups supported by your service provider until you find interesting-sounding ones with the **uk.** prefix.

There are hundreds of UK newsgroups to join, and they cover most common interests.

If a newsgroup that you know exists isn't carried by your service provider, there are a couple of options available to you. The first is to send an email to technical support requesting that the newsgroup is added to the feed. As long as the group doesn't carry questionable content, there's no reason why the service provider shouldn't add it to its newsfeed. Second, you can access Usenet archives on the World Wide Web by going to **http://www.dejanews.com/**. Enter subjects you're interested in and relevant newsgroup postings appear. Archives of almost every newsgroup on the Web can be found at Deja News. If your service provider won't support your favourite groups, you should consider subscribing to an independent newsfeed such as Supernews Wren. For $90 a year (about £60) you can subscribe to the 30,000 plus newsgroups available from SuperNews. The SuperNews Web site is at **http://www.supernews.com/**.

Full Group List

32132 groups

uk.adverts.books
uk.adverts.computer
uk.adverts.other
uk.adverts.personals
uk.adverts.personals.gay-lesbian-bi
uk.adverts.stolen.announce
uk.adverts.stolen.d
uk.announce
uk.announce.d
uk.announce.events
uk.announce.events.d
uk.answers
uk.business.telework
uk.community.firefighting
uk.community.social-housing
uk.community.voluntary
uk.comp.klix
uk.comp.misc
uk.comp.os.linux
uk.comp.os.win95
uk.comp.sys.sun
uk.comp.training
uk.comp.vendors
uk.consultants
uk.current-events.general
uk.current-events.n-ireland
uk.d-iy
uk.education.16plus
uk.education.expeditions
uk.education.governors
uk.education.home-education
uk.education.maths
uk.education.misc
uk.education.schools-it
uk.education.staffroom
uk.education.teachers
uk.environment
uk.environment.conservation
uk.finance
uk.food+drink.archives
uk.food+drink.misc
uk.food+drink.real-ale
uk.food+drink.restaurants
uk.games.board

DESIGNING FOR THE WEB

There will probably come a time when you want to make your mark on the Web by designing your own Web site. With our advice, you'll be able to create a site of wonder with the minimum of fuss

HOST WITH THE MOST

Q

We have already had a little Web site designed and we have registered a domain name with DNIC – bht.co.uk. The problem now is that we do not have the foggiest idea about who we should go approach to host it. It's a small site, less than a megabyte in size. We need unlimited forwarding from the registration forms for pupils and tutors to the postmaster and five different email addresses. We also want to record the number of people who visit the site. Can you offer us any advice?

A

If you already have an account with a service provider, you'll find that it will probably be able to set you up with a Web site using your own domain name. But you will be charged a fee for this service.

Alternatively, you can rent Web space from one of the many companies that offer users this kind of service.

NetDirect (**http://www.netdirect.com/**) offers a 10Mb package for £30 per quarter, or you could try ABA.NET (**http://aba.net/**) which offers a 6Mb package costing £99 per year plus a set-up fee.

aba.net

Welcome to aba.net

Low cost international web hosting with unlimited bandwidth and email forwarding

Friday 19 June, 1998

EXPLORER BIAS

Q

I have designed my Web site using FrontPage 97, which puts almost everything into frames, even blocks of plain text. Well, I can live with that, and I've also added a page counter at the bottom. But what magic HTML script do I need to write to get the best results in Netscape Navigator, as well as in Internet Explorer 3?

A

It depends what you want to do. Obviously, Web content created by a Microsoft application such as MS Publisher or FrontPage will be biased towards looking best in Internet Explorer. I don't know if anyone else has noticed, but HTML files created by Publisher and FrontPage contain reams of redundant commands that are unnecessary for the layout of the page, and make the file size needlessly large. I once reduced the file size of a page created in FrontPage 97 from 43kb to 11kb by removing the unnecessary code – and it looked exactly the same on the screen.

In the case of your page, the first <TABLE> command creates a row of about 25 cells, varying in width from one pixel to 60 pixels, none of them with any content. This is simply excess data that is not required by your page.

You may be better off loading your page in a plain text editor, stripping out all of the <TABLE> commands and using <CENTER>, <P>, <BR> and <HR> commands to format the page.

For true cross-browser compatibility, you need to use an independent HTML tool such as HoTMetaL PRO or Claris HomePage, and you'll need to get yourself a good HTML 3.2 text book to study the differences between Netscape's interpretation of HTML and Microsoft's version.

If you go to Waterstones or any book shop with a reasonable computer section, you should be able to pick up an HTML book for around £20.

I WANT MY FTP

Q I have two questions that I think you can help with. I have written my first ever Web Page for a local Football Club and I currently use the Web Publishing Wizard that comes with Internet Explorer to upload my files to the Web. I would like to see exactly what is on my site, to check if there is anything that I can delete. I believe that I need an FTP program to do this. Can you recommend a good but cheap one (free would be better) for me? My second query concerns Internet Explorer 4, which I have one main problem with. When I use the History part of the application to review recently-visited sites, I get the message that this site is not available offline. I have checked, and my history folder is set to delete only after 21 days. In my Temporary Internet folder options, I have set it to allow me to allocate two per cent of my hard drive (40Mb). Why can I sometimes not view old sites that I visited earlier on the same day?

A The first part of your problem is easy – use WS_FTP or FTP Explorer. Both programs will let you view the files at your Web site. While the Web Publishing Wizard is great for uploading files to the Web site, that's all you can do with it.

The second part of your question also has a relatively simple solution. Many Web pages, especially those hosted on servers using Microsoft Windows NT server software, create Web pages 'on the fly.' This means that the pages are created specifically to be downloaded to your browser when you visit the site, and are not stored as permanent files. Consequently, these pages cannot be stored and viewed offline.

Other pages may use graphics or data downloaded from other sites, or active content created on the server. Again, these pages cannot usually be viewed offline.

COUNT ON ME

With a little help, I have now completed my Web site and published it on the free 3Mb of space provided with my Global Internet account. I want to know if it will be worth the effort to make regular updates, based on the number of visitors to the site. Therefore, I want to place a counter on the site before I advertise it.

I've hit a major brick wall, however. I can find no advice, software or guidance explaining how I achieve this task. At great expense, I purchased six back issues of a mainstream PC magazine to obtain the 'build your own site' tutorial, but it conveniently misses hit counters out of the instructions. Very annoying, as you can imagine.

Don't worry – there's a simple cure. You can get a hit counter along with full instructions on how to set it up. And it's free! Go to the WebCounters page at **http://www.digits.com/**, where there's a free and a paid-for Web counter service. I've been using their counters for a couple of years without problems.

WebTrends - Click here for a free download

- Check Out the A2Z Top-10 Lists
- Plus Services Online

Your source for free and pay-for-use Web Auditing and Counting services.

[Create | Change | Query | HELP]
[News | Top 10 Sites | Advertising | Commercial]

 Net Digits ™ WebCounter ™ Copyright 1996. All Rights Reserved.
For comments or questions, please see the Feedback Page.
http://www.digits.com/.

SMALL IS BEAUTIFUL

Q I'm thinking of putting a professional Web site together and I'm a little concerned that the graphics files I want to use are too large. How can I compress my GIF and JPEG images for the best results, without losing too much quality? I don't want to put people off visiting my pages by making them too large.

A There are a couple of options open to you. If you want a professional quality product, you should take a look at GEO's WebCharger, which is capable of reducing images to a quarter of the file size of standard JPEG images. WebCharger can compress JPEG, PICT, GIF and BMP images, and outputs the final image in a JPEG compatible format that can be viewed in any Web browser. WebCharger costs £49 from Principal Distribution (**01756 704000**) for Windows and Macintosh. The GEO home page is at **http://www.emblaze.com/**.

The other alternative is GIF Wizard, an online service that scans the GIF images on your Web pages and compresses them more efficiently. GIF Wizard is an excellent product, and it can even compress animated GIFs. The charges for using GIF Wizard vary, and you can get full details from the site at **http://www.gifwizard.com/**.

ON TARGET

I have designed a set of Web pages using a text editor. It is structured as a start/index page without any frames, but with links that you can click on. Clicking on a link takes you to a page using frames. I have added an icon in the frame to take you back to the original start page. The problem I am having is that when returning to the opening start page it is loaded into the frame, and not as a standalone page. What can I do about this? Is it something to do with the TARGET part of the command?

You are correct when you suggest the problem may lie with the TARGET parameter in the link command. To force a page to load into a full page window in a Web browser you must add the TARGET=''_top'' parameter to the link, one of the Magic TARGET Names.

Say that your link from the framed pages looks like this:
<A HREF=''index.htm''>Index page></A>

To open a full-screen window you have to change it as follows:
<A HREF=''index.htm'' TARGET=''_top''>Index page></A>

Here's a list of the four Magic TARGET Names you can use in frames.

TARGET=''_blank'' forces the document referenced in the <A> tag to be loaded into a new unnamed window.

TARGET=''_self'' causes the document referred to in the <A> tag to be loaded into the frame containing the link.

TARGET=''_parent'' forces the link to load into the <FRAMESET> parent of the current document. If the document has no parent, TARGET=''_self'' is used.

TARGET=''_top'' forces the document referenced in the <A> tag to be loaded into a new full-screen window without frames.

And that's it – problem solved.

HTML BREAKDOWN

Q   **I want to lay out text on a Web page in paragraphs separated by tabbed indents (as in a word-processed document) rather than by blank lines. The <p>, or paragraph, tab always leaves a blank line. Help!**

A   It's pretty simple really. Instead of the paragraph tag you use the break tag, <br>. However, tabs are a little more awkward. In many ways it's better to use a hard space, like so:

   Use three or four of these instead of a tab to maintain a consistent look to the text in your Web page.

PICTURE THIS

If I save pictures from Web pages on my PC and then double-click on them, Paint Shop Pro [a popular picture editing program for the PC – Ed.] will open some of them but Internet Explorer opens others. Paint Shop Pro says it doesn't recognise the file format of those Internet Explorer opens. How can I tell what the file format is and can you explain what's happening?

Oh yes. And we will. First, though, let's change Windows 95 so it shows filetypes. Open Internet Explorer and from the View menu select 'Options.' On the first page of the dialog box unselect 'Hide MS-DOS filetypes for file types that are registered' and while you're about it, select 'Show all files.' The filetypes referred to are the three letters after the final dot in a DOS filename, which you can now see. Most of the images you're saving off Web pages are going to have a JPG filetype. However, on Mac and Unix systems, the JPG filetype is usually written as JPEG (which is correct but has four letters, so is an illegal filename under DOS – DOS restricts you to an 8.3 format).

Since Windows 95 came out, there have been few restrictions on file names, and Win95 will happily accept long filetypes as

well (don't worry, we're getting there). If you look at the image files you've downloaded, you'll find some have a JPG filetype and some a JPEG filetype. Many Windows programs throw up their hands at this – apart from Web browsers. Select a file with a JPEG filetype and click it again to edit it. Change it to JPG and Paint Shop Pro will now open it. In a related problem, installing Internet Explorer will often change the file associations – which means the program Windows 95 uses to open a file when you double-click on it can change. Re-installing the program you want to use is the quickest fix. Alternatively, you can simply drag the file using the mouse and drop it on the program you want to use.

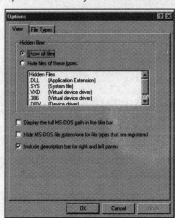

LEGAL EAGLE

Q I've read some news stories recently about people being sued for having links to other Web sites from their home pages. How can this be illegal? I thought this was the whole point of the Web.

A The fuss is largely over 'framed' sites passing off other content as their own – by showing it in a frame surrounded by their own titles, navigation and so on. Naturally, most people who put up Web pages want as many links to it as possible in order to gain an audience – otherwise, as you

say, there's no point. However, another frowned-upon activity is linking directly to graphics or other content on someone else's site within your own Web page without gaining permission. It's also pretty stupid as changes on the site you're linking to can break your pages. Don't do it, but don't worry about the usual kind of links to pages with related content, for example.

WHAT IS XML?

A friend of mine said I should be looking into coding with XML. At first I thought he was winding me up, but I have seen it mentioned in several magazines. But what is XML and where can I find out more about using it?

XML stands for Extensible Markup Language and it's designed to provide a universal format for storing data on the Internet; the World Wide Web specifically. XML enables Web site developers to create pages of structured data taken from any application and display it on a Web page.

XML will complement HTML, but it doesn't replace it. Internet Explorer 4 already supports Microsoft's implementation of XML.

You can find out more about XML, and its associated style-sheet sub-set XSL on the Microsoft Web site at **http://www. microsoft.com/xml**.

A very good book about XML is Professional Style Sheets for HTML and XML published by WROX, ISBN 1-861001-65-7, priced at £37.49. It's a very comprehensive book and covers CSS1, CSS2, XML and XSL.

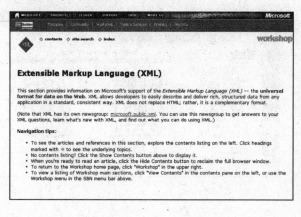

MUSIC PLEASE

Q

I thought it would be a great idea to have some suitable music as a welcome to my Web site at **http://www. service-pals.clara.net/**. I created a suitably themed WAV file for the first page in each section of the site: the Army, the RAF and the Navy. But now the files take too long to download to be effective in the browser. I thought it would be a good idea to convert the WAV files to MIDI format so they download faster and produce the right ambience for the page.

But I have unable to find a program that converts WAV to MIDI format.

A

I've spent a while trawling the Web for the kind of utility you want, and I have found something at a US company called Wildcat Canyon Software, which you'll find at **http://www. wildcat.com**. Wildcat sells a couple of programs that can do what you want, but they're not cheap. Autoscore Pro weighs in at $249 (£160) and Autoscore Deluxe 2.0 is a little cheaper at $119 (£75). You can order these products online, and pay by credit card.

TAG WRESTLING

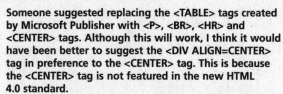

Q Someone suggested replacing the <TABLE> tags created by Microsoft Publisher with <P>, <BR>, <HR> and <CENTER> tags. Although this will work, I think it would have been better to suggest the <DIV ALIGN=CENTER> tag in preference to the <CENTER> tag. This is because the <CENTER> tag is not featured in the new HTML 4.0 standard.

And now here's a tip that will help speed up download times. Using the Display control panel in Windows 95, set your screensaver and wallpaper settings to none. This is a particularly good tip for users who have a limited amount of RAM installed – it can almost double your download rates.

A You're almost right when you say that the <CENTER> tag isn't supported in HTML 4.0 – the <CENTER> tag is being deprecated in favour of style sheets. But so is the <DIV ALIGN=CENTER> tag. In fact, the <CENTER> tag is an abbreviation of <DIV ALIGN=CENTER>, as both tags perform the same function.

It's worth noting that while many of the commands in the HTML 3.2 specification are being deprecated in HTML 4.0, when a tag is deprecated, it basically means that the tag is 'no longer approved of' rather than replaced outright. Netscape Navigator/Communicator 5 and Internet Explorer 5 will be fully compatible with all HTML 3.2 commands as well as supporting the new HTML 4.0 specification.

If you are serious about learning HTML 4.0, the best book I've found so far is Teach Yourself Web Publishing With HTML 4 from SAMS.NET, ISBN 1-57521-305-2.

It's rather expensive at £54.95 but it's the most comprehensive HTML 4.0 reference I've seen.

MISCELLANEOUS NET TIPS

This is the section of
the book where all the
Net niggles normally
overlooked are solved

LAST OF THE BBS FANS

Q I recently purchased the McAfee VirusScan Suite. The acknowledgement on the registration said that I can get upgrades via McAfee's Bulletin Board System. The documentation includes a phone number, login name and password, but I'm not sure how to connect to the BBS. I have tried using my Netscape Navigator browser from Virgin Net and dialling up the BBS number but nothing happens. What am I doing wrong?

A An easy one to cure, this. Your mistake is trying to use an Internet Web browser to connect to a bulletin board service (BBS). BBSs have nothing to do with the Internet – they are closed systems you connect to using special communications software. You cannot connect to BBSs using Internet-based software, you need a terminal program.

But you can get the updates you need from the World Wide Web. McAfee has its own Web site at **http://www.mcafee.com/**.

When the page opens, click on the 'Download' button in the top menu. Click on the 'Product Updates' button on the next page, then select the 'Virus Updates' button. Now all you have to do is click on the Virus DAT file you want to download.

NOT A SOUND

Q

When I was using the Internet this week, I came to a section that allows me to select audio/video. When I select this option, my computer responds with the message 'Windows cannot find Pnclient.exe.' I have tried to locate this file on my computer using the Find utility, but it is not there. Is there anywhere I can get a copy of this file?

A

This message normally crops up if you are trying to use the older version of the RealNetworks RealAudio software with AOL. The solution is relatively simple if you already have the RealAudio software installed on your PC. Use Windows Explorer to explore your hard drive and locate the RAPLAYER folder. Inside, find the file called RAPLAYER.EXE and change its name to PNCLIENT.EXE.

Another solution would be to download the latest version of RealPlayer from the RealNetworks site at **http://www. realnetworks.com**.

PARANOID ANDROID

Q If one installs Microsoft software 'borrowed' from a friend, and not personally bought, is it possible for Microsoft to check by use of 'cookies' or other technical wizardry that you are illegally using the program?

And does it make any difference if I am with MSN – is it easier to check on the software installed? I am, by the way, well aware of the copyright law. As a reader of *Practical Internet* from issue one, can you once and for all settle this argument.

A There was a lot of fuss about this issue when Windows 95 was launched. It is certainly possible to create programs or ActiveX components that can read the directory of your hard drive, list the software installed on your PC and upload a list of them over the Internet while you are online. And the serial numbers could be checked to see if the software is registered to you. But does this actually happen, does Microsoft do this? The answer is – probably – no. This kind of action contravenes laws such as the Data Protection Act, and this kind of information about a system can only be uploaded voluntarily by the owner of the PC in question. Being a member of MSN would not make too much difference, as this kind of sniffer program could be installed on any page on the Internet.

WHO RUNS THE NET?

Q If the Internet is not regulated, as is often mentioned, how do countries obtain their abbreviated names in URLs, such as xyz.co.uk? Who do countries approach for the name, and is the application done by any one organisation or by national governments?

A Although the Internet is widely regarded as unregulated, this usually refers to Web content and censorship, rather than the standards and protocols used by computer systems to move information about. Non-profit organisations such as the World Wide Web Consortium at **http://www.w3c.org**, Network Solutions at **http://www.netsol.com/** and other bodies actually thrash out the details of communications protocols, domain names and so on.

Domain names were originally assigned by the Internet International Ad-Hoc Committee (IAHC) at **http://www.iahc.org/**.

Now, however, the IAHC has been disbanded and replaced by – wait for it – the Generic Top Level Domain Memorandum of Understanding (gTLD-MoU), which deals with domain name questions. The gTLD-MoU is at **http://www.gtld-mou.org/**.

There are several other organisations which play a part in running the Net. The Internet Engineering Task Force (**http://www.ietf.org/**) works on new, faster Internet protocols, such as the new IPng (Internet Protocol next generation), and the Internet Society, at **http://www.isoc.org/**, is an international organisation devoted to global co-operation and co-ordination for the Internet. The World Wide Web consortium (W3C), is one of the better known Net bodies, and works on Web protocols and standards.

W3C WORLD WIDE WEB

Leading the Web to its Full Potential...

W3C Issues Accessibility Guidelines to Extend Benefits of the Web to a Broader Community

"The WAI Page Authoring Guidelines reflect the accessibility improvements in HTML, 4.0, and are an outcome of a collaboration among industry, disability and research organizations, as well as governments from around the world."
– Judy Brewer, Director of the Web Accessibility Initiative (WAI) International Program Office

Catch the W3C Track at WWW7, the Seventh International World Wide Web Conference April 14-18, 1998

now available - -

• version 1.2 release of Amaya, W3C's WYSIWYG testbed Web editor/browser, in both Unix and Windows versions
• two new, simultaneous releases of Jigsaw, W3C's award-winning,

User Interface

HTML
Style Sheets
Synchronized Virtual Media
Math
Graphics
Internationalization
Fonts
Amaya

Technology and Society

Digital Signature Initiative
Metadata
P3P
Privacy (P3P)
Electronic Commerce

Architecture

HTTP
HTTP-NG
Standardized Multimedia

SMART FTP

Q

I would like a recommendation for a good FTP program. I use Lotus SmartSuite and it seems to have a built-in FTP utility to use if you author your pages with WordPro. Would this be suitable, or would I need a third party FTP program to upload files to my Web site?

A

I don't use SmartSuite myself, but if it has an FTP client built in, I see no reason not to use it. Personally, I use WS_FTP. I know there are newer FTP applications around, but I like WS_FTP because it's so easy to use. You can download a free version by pointing your browser at **http://www.ipswitch.com/**, and it works on Windows 95 and Windows 3.1.

Another good FTP program for Windows 95 is FTP Explorer, and you can get it from **http://ftpx.com/**.

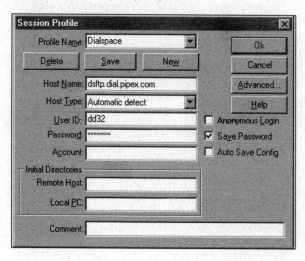

I NAME THAT SITE IN...

 Could you please advise me if there is an alternative method for me to register a domain name, rather than getting my service provider to do it for me?

You could go directly to Network Solutions at **http://www.internic.net/**, but you have to provide details about the administration of your domain name, where it's going to be hosted and so on. A simpler solution is to use a domain name registration service. One of the best, and one of the less expensive services, is provided by DomNames.com at **http://www.domnames.com/**.

It costs £65 to register through DomNames.com, plus there is a $100 fee from InterNIC for the first two years' administration of your domain name. You can use the online form on the DomNames Web site, or call DomNames on **01703 864422**. Other services, such as email forwarding and Web space rental are also available.

MAGIC NUMBER

Q

I was asked the other night on Yahoo! chat if I had an ICQ number. Please explain what it is and how I can obtain one.

A

It's a seven figure number and it's also your ICQ address, a bit like an email address or street address. ICQ itself is an Instant Chat program from a company called Mirabilis

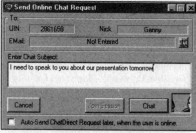

(http://www.mirabilis.com). You can try out ICQ from our cover CD. It works in the same way as the AOL Messenger, automatically informing you when friends log on to the Net (assuming you're logged on yourself), allowing you to flash up a message to them on their screen. Of course, they can do the same to you – in fact anyone with your ICQ number can call you online. ICQ is extremely popular among children and teenagers, but less so with older Net users. There are now half a dozen or so mutually incompatible instant chat utilities out there. Just what the world needs – more standards!

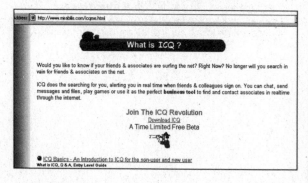

NET TELEPHONY

Q Is there a piece of software that allows you to phone anywhere in the world through your service provider at local rates? For example, first log on to your service provider, then load the correct software, type in the phone number you want and make a call?

A No, not in quite the way you mean. Or yes, but not in quite the way you mean. Getting your voice call onto the Net is easy, and there are plenty of PC-to-PC (and to other computers) Net telephony programs. Microsoft gives away a very good one called NetMeeting as part of Internet Explorer. Unfortunately, getting your voice from the Net onto the PSTN (Public Service Telephone Network) – and hence to an ordinary telephone – requires a special kind of Internet gateway machine, which someone will charge you to use. In practice, the commercial version of this technique enables you to make cheap calls from your phone to another phone – usually in another country – with the call automatically routed over private parts of the Net. You just don't realise it. You use a special number to access the service and then tap in the phone number you want. A good example is Deutsche Telekom, which has a UK branch. The company has a technology called T-NetCall which you can use to cheaply phone people over the Net in the USA, Australia and 18 other countries in Europe and the Far East. Deutsche Telekom is planning to add fax and – this is the bit you want – telephoning from PC to telephone. Check the service out on the Web at **http://www. t-netcall.berkom.de**. Eventually, all voice calls will use Internet-style packet switching because it's dramatically cheaper.

THE COMPLETE INTERNET GLOSSARY

The place to turn to when you're faced with baffling acronyms and jargon. Keep this next to your PC and never be short of an answer. Supplied by New Media in Business Ltd (http://www.nmib.com)

ActiveX

A set of technologies that enables software components to interact with one another in a networked environment. It was developed by Microsoft and is currently administered as a Standard by the Open Group. In the context of the Internet, it is used for interactive components that add extra functionality to Web Sites, for a similar purpose to Applets.

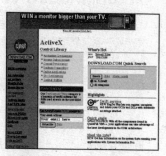

ActiveX add increased interactivity to Web sites

See also: Applet.

AltaVista

One of the most popular search engines. The Web address is **http://www.altavista.digital.com**. See also: Search engines.

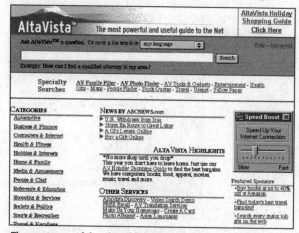

The most powerful and useful guide to the Net (allegedly)

Anonymous FTP

Anonymous File Transfer Protocol. A mechanism for moving files from a user machine to, or from, a remote Internet machine

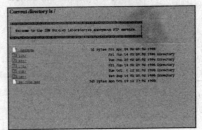

anonymously. In other words, you do not have to identify yourself with a user name or password. See also: FTP.

Recluses and hermits alike use anonymous FTP

Applet

A small program that runs 'in a browser.' Applets are usually written in Java. They differ from applications in that they have restricted functionality that is designed to protect the users machine from faulty or malicious code. The restrictions include the inability to write to the user's hard disk, or execute operating system functions. The applets are downloaded from Web sites along with the Web page in which it was embedded. They are typically used to provide a more advanced user interface than HTML is capable of.

See also: ActiveX, Java.

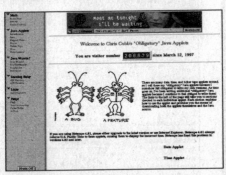

An applet a day keeps the doctor away. Well, that's the theory

Archie

A system for finding files which are stored on anonymous FTP sites.

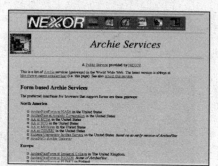

Archie helps you track down stored files. What a decent chap he is

ARPANET

Advanced Research Projects Agency Network and the precursor to the Internet. It was created in 1969 by the US Department of Defence to conduct research into networking.

See also: Internet.

Charles Babbage Institute
Center for the History of Information Processing

The IMP Development Group (left to right): Truett Thatch, Bill Bartell, Jim Geisman, Dave Walden, Frank Heart, Ben Barker, Marty Thrope, Will Crowther, Severo Ornstein, and Bob Kahn (c. 1970, photo courtesy of BBN Systems and Technologies).

25th Anniversary of ARPANET

CBI examined the history of the ARPANET as part of its project for the Defense Advanced Research Projects Agency on the History of the Information Processing Techniques Office. The ARPANET history is one chapter in the forthcoming book by Arthur L. Norberg and Judy E. O'Neill with contributions by Kerry Freedman. The Johns Hopkins University Press recently accepted the manuscript for publication in 1995.

Twenty-five years ago the Advanced Research Projects Agency (ARPA) began to construct a resource sharing computer network among its contractors. This network became known as the ARPANET, a wildly successful wide-area packet-switching network which later evolved into the Internet.

By the middle 1960s, the Information Processing Techniques Office (IPTO) of ARPA had computing research activities underway across the continental United States. The contractors used different computer systems including some that were unique, such as the Project MAC system at MIT and the developing ILLIAC IV supercomputer at the University of Illinois. An effective connection between the machines would allow IPTO to fund a large system in one location and have it economically used without regard to the physical location of the machine or the researcher.

Did you celebrate the 25th anniversary of Arpanet? Thought not

Avatar

An image such as a human figure or face that users choose to represent themselves in an online chat forum.

See also: Chat Forum.

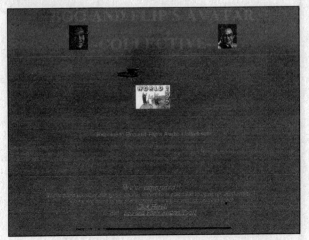

If you fancy an online image makeover, pop along to Boo and Flip

Backbone

A path through a network (such as the Internet) that has a very high capacity. By taking a large part of the network traffic over large distances, it helps to speed up the network as a whole.

See also: Network.

Save bandwidth at the Bandwidth Conservation Society (http://www.infohiway.com/faster)

Bandwidth

A measure of how much data can be transmitted down any connection. For example a normal telephone line with the latest modems has a bandwidth of 56,000 bits per second.

See also: Bps, Bit.

Baud

The baud rate of a modem is a measure of how many bits it can send or receive per second. Each baud is equal to 4 bits per second. So a 600 baud modem would process data at 2,400 bits per second.

See also: Bit, Modem.

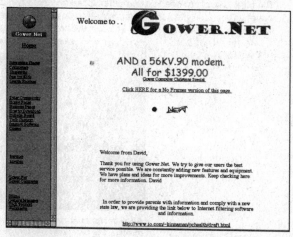

When David isn't commenting on cricket, he sells modems

Binaries

In the context of newsgroups, the term binary is used to refer to images/photographs that are attached to an email message. More generally, it is a term used in computing to describe files which do not consist of text.

```
alt.binaries.3d.bryce
alt.binaries.3d.lightwave
alt.binaries.GDi-Land
alt.binaries.SR.repost
alt.binaries.X
alt.binaries.activism.militia
alt.binaries.allmanbrothers
alt.binaries.amiga
alt.binaries.andrew.lloyd-webber
alt.binaries.anna-nicole-smith
alt.binaries.anna-nicole.smith
alt.binaries.applications.mac
alt.binaries.astronomy
alt.binaries.atari
alt.binaries.atari.cancelbots
alt.binaries.atari.d
alt.binaries.atari.dead
```

Bit

The basic unit of storage in a computer. It can only hold two values a 0 or 1. All data stored in computers – numbers, letters, images, etc are made up on bits. Bit is derived from Binary Digit. A byte consists of 8 bits.

See also: Bps, Byte Bot.

All data stored in computers consists of bits – the basic unit of storage – pictures, text, whatever...

3Com is just one example of a company that makes modems. There are many more

Bps

Bits per second. A measurement of speed of data transfer from one place to another. For example, a 56,000bps modem can process 56,000 bits per second.

See also: Bandwidth, Bit.

Browser

A software tool which accesses Web sites, obtains Web pages and displays them on the screen. It is also used to support other Internet resources.

More details on this subject are available in the online version of the HyperGlossary (**http://www.hyperglossary.co.uk**).

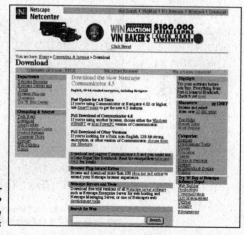

Netscape or Explorer? The decision is yours

Byte

The standard unit of measure for computer storage. It is the unit that holds a single character (in Western Alphabets) such as the letter 'A' or the dollar sign '$.' Languages such as Chinese and Japanese use two or more bytes for each character. Each byte

consists of 8 bits to represent the character and one or more bits for internal computer purposes.

See also: Bit, Kilobyte, Megabyte, Gigabyte, Terabyte.

Why is Whatis.com definition of something so small just so long?

Cache

In the context of the Web, the term is used to refer to an area on a computer's disk that is used to store files (Web pages, images, etc) that have been downloaded from a Web site for you to view in your browser. The files are stored so that if you want to view the pages or images later, they can be presented far more quickly – without waiting for them to be downloaded a second time.

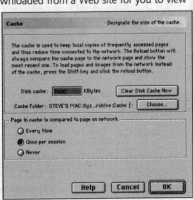

Cover your tracks on the Internet by regularly clearing out your disk cache

Cascading Style Sheets (CSS)

A mechanism for specifying the style of a Web page separately from the Web page. The benefit is that the look and feel of a set of Web pages can be amended by altering one file that contains the style rather than having to edit each of the Web pages.

Using Cascading Style Sheets can save you lot of time when updating a site

Certificate

A document that is used to certify that a user or organisation are who they say they are. They contain information about who it belongs to, who it was issued by, expiry date and information that can be used to check out the contents of the certificate. It is as an important part of the SSL system for establishing secure connections.

See also: Certificate Authority, SSL.

Check a certificate to find out if a company is who it says it is on the Internet

Certificate Authority

An authority that issues
certificates needed to
authenticate users or
organisations on the Internet.
See also: Certificate, SSL.

*A certificate wouldn't be any
good if it couldn't be
authenticated, now would it?*

CGI

Common Gateway Interface. A set of rules for how programs can
communicate with Web Server software. Programs that run on a
Web Server and use the common gateway interface are called
CGI programs.

CGI programs are written to process data that the Web user
types into a form on a Web Page. They send results back to the
user by generating a Web page and passing it to the Web Server
software. CGI programs can be used to provide databases
querying and updating facilities on Web sites.

Many Web Servers provide their own version of CGI. For
example, ISAPI
can be used
with Microsoft
Internet
Information
Server. It runs
faster than
CGI but will
not work with
all other web
servers.
See also: Web
Server.

*What's common, not invented in Essex and allows
a program to communicate?*

Channel

A Web site that automatically downloads information to your computer according to a pre-arranged schedule.

This is also referred to as Push Technology.

Chat Forum

A group of Internet users exchanging messages on a subject of common interest. Unlike newsgroups, all the participants are connected to the forum at the same time and the messages are displayed immediately for members of the forum to see.

Client

A client machine is a computer that operates by obtaining some information or service from another machine – a server. For example your machine with a Web browser on is a client machine. To obtain Web pages, the browser goes to a Web server machine. The software that supports the operation of the client is known as client software.
See also: Server.

Your humble PC with a Web browser on can be described as a client machine. Amazing!

Client/Server

A client/server system is one where the users computer (the client) works with another computer (the server) in order to achieve the desired results. This contrasts with the traditional mainframes

where everything is done on the mainframe with the (dumb) terminals simply displaying the results. The World Wide Web is a Client/Server system with the browser on the client computer requesting Web pages from the Web Server machine.

Cookies are often used on shopping sites to keep a list of what you've bought

Cookie

A piece of information sent by a Web Server to a browser for storage on the client machine. The browser sends the information back to the Web Server when the latter requests it. This mechanism is used because the Web Server has no way of recognising a particular user when they revisit the site. In fact if you link from one page on the site to another on the same Web Site, the Web Server would not know that it is the same user looking at the two pages.

On sites that you log on to, cookies are used to hold your id and password (so you don't have to log on each page!) On shopping sites the cookie could be used to keep a list of what you have bought so far, so that you can choose things as you see them rather than having to restate what you want when you get to the checkout.

Crawler

A Web Crawler (or Spider) is a piece of software that scans the World Wide Web finding pages to add to the index of a search engine.
See also: Search Engines.

Directories

A World Wide Web directory is a Web Site that is used to locate Web sites and Web pages in predefined areas of interest. For each of these predefined areas, the directory provides a set of hypertext links to all the Web pages that fall within that area of interest.

Search directories like Yahoo! will find the sites you need in no time at all

More details on this subject are available in the online version of the HyperGlossary (**http://www.hyperglossary.co.uk**).

Discussion Group

An alternative name for the Newsgroups supported by Usenet.
See also: Usenet.

Messages 1-25 of exactly 2762 matches for search Freeserve:

	Date	Sz:	Subject	Newsgroup	Author
1.	98/11/12	027	Freeserve/Turnpike news coll	demon.ip.support.turn	Colin Barnes
2.	98/11/12	026	Re: Freeserve	uk.local.birmingham	------> BillyNO
3.	98/11/12	026	Getting A FreeServe UID	alt.internet.provider	Julian Wilkinso
4.	98/11/12	026	Re: Turnpike & Freeserve	demon.ip.support.turn	Chris Holmes
5.	98/11/12	026	V-90 With Demon but not with	demon.tech.modems	Chris Holmes
6.	98/11/11	026	ISP DNS address for Freeserv	intel.inbusiness	Richard Alberto
7.	98/11/11	026	Help! Can I access my Freese	alt.internet.provider	Hugh Janus
8.	98/11/11	026	Turnpike & Freeserve	demon.ip.support.turn	Richard Kemp
9.	98/11/10	026	Re: Turnpike & Freeserve	demon.ip.support.turn	Paul Terry
10.	98/11/10	025	Re: News collection with Tur	demon.ip.support.turn	Sam Sherret
11.	98/11/10	025	Re: Demon slower than Freese	demon.service.isdn	Nigel J. Carron
12.	98/11/10	025	Re: Bypassing Freeserve	uk.telecom	Graeme McKay
13.	98/11/10	025	Can't login to Freeserve any	demon.tech.modems	Graham Lunn
14.	98/11/10	025	Re: Competing with freeserve	demon.service	Phil Payne
15.	98/11/09	025	Re: Dixon's Freeserve compac	demon.ip.support.turn	Sam Sherret
16.	98/11/09	025	Re: Connect to freeserve wit	comp.sys.psion.comm	Rob Crossland
17.	98/11/09	025	Re: Demon slower than Freese	demon.service.isdn	Lawrence Kirby
18.	98/11/09	025	Re: IE4 provided by freeserv	uk.comp.os.win95	Dave Stanton
19.	98/11/08	025	Login Scripts for Freeserve	alt.winsock.trumpet	John A Grove
20.	98/11/08	025	Freeserve users	alt.fan.oksana-bayul.	Jeffrey
21.	98/11/08	025	News collection with Turnpik	demon.ip.support.turn	kym
22.	98/11/08	025	MS Messaging with Freeserve?	alt.internet.provider	R.B. Smissaert
23.	98/11/07	025	Freeserve - cant connect..	alt.internet.provider	Joe Curry
24.	98/11/07	025	Freeserve - service provider	comp.sys.mac.misc	ALeon83677
25.	98/11/06	025	Connect to freeserve with g5	comp.sys.psion.comm	Arijit Sadhu (

There are thousands of discussion groups which cover every subject you could possibly imagine – and then some...

Domain Name

The domain name is the name that uniquely identifies organisations on the Internet. For example **ual.com** is the domain name of United Airlines, **royal.gov.uk** is the domain name of the British Royal family and my company is **nmib.com**. You will encounter them most frequently in Web addresses, mine is **http://www.nmib.com/**, and email addresses – mine is **John@nmib.com**.

See also: Email, URL.

Type in http://www.paragon.co.uk into a browser location box and you will be taken to the Paragon Publishing site

Ecommerce

Electronic Commerce is conducting commerce over the Internet, such as buying products or services from Web sites.

Electronic Commerce has yet to take off in the UK due to worries about security

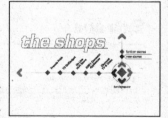

Encryption

Encoding information before it is transmitted over the Internet so that no one else can read it except the computer that it is sent to.

Email

Electronic Mail is a mechanism for sending messages across a computer network. The text of the message is typed in on one computer and then is sent to someone else on the network. The recipient

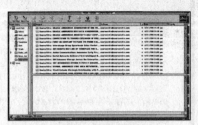

Programs such as Netscape Messenger make writing emails a dream

of the message reads it on his/her computer and can then delete the message, file it on the computer, print it, send a reply or forward it to other people on the network. Email is the standard abbreviation for Electronic Mail.

You can also use mailing lists to send a single message to many other users at the same time.

More details on this subject are available in the online version of the HyperGlossary (**http://www.hyperglossary.co.uk**).

Extranet

You are not Authorized for this Area

We are sorry, but you are not authorized to view stories in the Internet wire. If you do not have a subscription, please subscribe now. If you already have a subscription for this wire, please go back and check your username and password to make sure you entered them correctly. Thank You.

Internet | Telecom | Computers | Networks | Asia IT | Website Reviews
Home | Subscribe | About Newsbytes | Meet The Editors | Feedback | Search

Copyright (c) Post-Newsweek Business Information, Inc. All rights reserved.
For more Newsbytes see http://www.newsbytes.com

Access to an extranet is restricted by use of a password

An extranet is a private site which is accessed by a limited group of users over the Internet. Access to Extranet sites is restricted by password or other means.
More details on this subject are available in the online version of the HyperGlossary (**http://www. hyperglossary.co.uk**).

E-zine

An electronic magazine – in other words a magazine on the Web.

FAQs

Frequently Asked Questions. A set of questions with associated answers which set out to shed light on a particular subject area.

Fire Wall

A computer system that is used to prevent users on the Internet from getting unauthorised access to a LAN. See also: LAN.

Flame Mail

Electronic Mail of an angry and often abusive nature. Typically sent to an Internet user who breaks the rules of one of the newsgroups, for example, advertising when in a group that forbids it.

Freeware

Software that is available free of charge. If software is free of charge for a limited (trial) period it is called shareware.

You can get some good software on the Net and some of it is even free

FTP

CuteFTP is a great piece shareware which allows you to upload Web pages

File Transfer Protocol. A mechanism for moving files between two machines over the Internet. An FTP site is a collection of documents, software, etc. which Internet users can transfer to their computers using FTP. The term 'anonymous ftp' is used to refer to sites where no user id or password is needed to access the files. In other words, the users are anonymous. FTP is also commonly used to transfer Web pages from the Webmaster's machine to the Web Server.

More details on this subject are available in the online version of the HyperGlossary (**http://www.hyperglossary.co.uk**).

Fuzzy Logic

A technique for matching items that are similar. For example, if you are using a search engine to find pages containing references to Stephen Thomson using fuzzy logic, it might well return pages that contain Stephen Thompson, Steven Thomson and Steven Thompson as well.

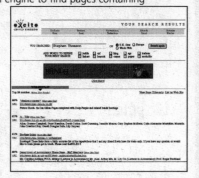

Believe it or not, there is a logic to the madness when you search for a site

GIF

Graphic Interchange Format. One of the two standard formats used for image files on the Internet. The other standard format is JPEG. GIF format is well suited to diagrams and human created pictures and diagrams. It is also possible to do simple animations with the Animated GIF format.

See also: JPEG.

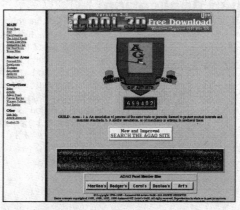

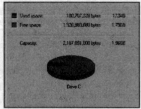

Right-click your hard drive icon for its size in Gigabytes

Gigabyte

1,000 Megabytes, that is 1,000,000,000 bytes. The purists will tell you that it is actually the binary equivalent, which is 1024 x 1024 x 1024!
See also: Byte, Kilobyte, Megabyte, Terabyte.

Gopher

A predecessor of the World Wide Web which has been eclipsed by the latter's arrival. It works by providing a menu of hyperlinks that you can select from. This often leads to another menu which you select from until you eventually reach the document you were seeking. It is still used widely in the academic world.

See also: WWW, Hypertext.

Helper Application

An application that is used to process a file format that the browser cannot handle. Typically used for multimedia files and animations. Since there is an overhead in calling helper applications, plugs-ins are used for the most commonly used formats. Plug-ins fulfil the same function as helper applications, but they are in effect made part of the browser itself.
See also: Plug-in.

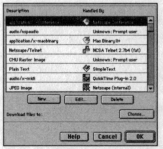

Hit

A hit count is used as a measure of the popularity of a Web Page. One is added to the hit count every time anyone reads the page. Some pages publish their hit counts. The hit count for a Web Site is the sum of all the hit counts for each file that makes up

Revealing that your site only got three hits in the last year is not a good idea

the Web. This is used to measure the overall popularity of the Web Site and the load on the Web Server.

Home Page

A home page is the starting point for browsing a set of Web pages. Every Web Site has a home page that is designed to be the first page seen. It typically has links to the various parts of the Web Site. A Browser also has a home page – the one that is displayed automatically when you invoke the browser. The leading browsers let you choose your own home page. This

means you can ensure that your starting point is your favourite search engine, directory or the home page of your own Web Site if you have one. The term is also used for a Web page created by an individual to say who they are and describe their interests, etc – e.g. Jane Smith's home page.

A browser has a home page which kicks in when you connect to the Net

Host

A computer on a network. The term is sometimes used to refer to computers that offer services to other computers such as running a Web Service or a Database.

Demon is just one company that acts as a host

HTML is the basis of all pages on the Internet. Luckily we don't usually have to read this

HTML

HyperText Markup Language. The language used to create Web pages. It consists of a set of tags which indicate what action the browser should take when loading and processing the page. For example, the horizontal rule <hr> causes a horizontal line to appear.
There are also HTML tags for incorporating graphics into the file and for defining hyperlinks.

HTTP

HyperText Transport Protocol. The language that Web Browsers use to communicate with Web servers. You will no doubt recognise HTTP as a part the address of Web sites.
See also: Protocol.

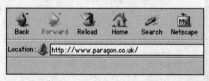

HyperGlossary

An invented term to describe the combination of definitions and concepts provided by New Media in Business Ltd (http://www.nmib.com).

Hyperlink

A hyperlink is part of a Web page that provides a link to another part of the World Wide Web. The words Link and Hypertext link are used interchangeably with hyperlink.

More details on this subject are available in the online version of the HyperGlossary (**http://www. hyperglossary.co.uk**).

Without links, getting around the Web would be a very slow process indeed

Hypertext

Text that contains hyperlinks to other documents. In other words, when the text is displayed you can click on certain regions of the document and are taken to elsewhere in the document or to another document. This is the basis of the World Wide Web.

See also: Hyperlink.

Win a brand new Peugeot 306XSi, or one of Twenty Adventure Days Out, in our Free Grand Prize Draw!

Id

A string of characters that identifies you, typically your name or initials, used when you are logging on to a computer system.
 See also: Logon/Login.

Anyone that uses a computer and Internet regularly has to remember an ever expanding list of passwords and ids

IETF

See: Internet Engineering Task Force.

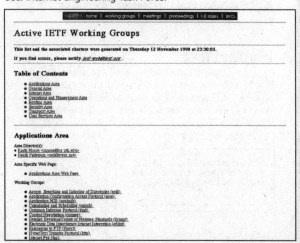

Internet

The Internet (with a capital I) is a vast network of computers that straddles the world which is open for anyone to join. It hosts the World Wide Web and provides an email connection for countless organisations and individuals. "internet" (with a lower case i) is a network that consists of two or more networks liked together. So the Internet is the most significant example of an internet.

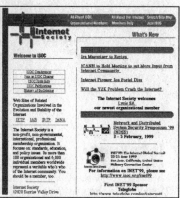

If you are searching for a history of the Web, see the Internet Society

Internet Engineering Task Force (IETF)

The body that is responsible for most of the Internet Standards. More details on this subject are available in the online version of the HyperGlossary (**http://www.hyperglossary.co.uk**) under Standards

No it's not the SAS, it's the Internet Engineering Task Force

Internet Service Provider

An Internet service provider is an organisation that offers Internet services including connection to the Internet and Web site hosting. Internet Service Providers are invariably referred to as ISPs.

Virgin Net is one of around 300 or so ISPs in the UK

Intranet

A private network that employs Internet Technology.

Usually the network will be restricted to a single organisation. The prime Internet technology that distinguishes an Intranet from a normal local area network is the use of the Web.

More details on this subject are available in the online version of the HyperGlossary (**http://www.hyperglossary.co.uk**).

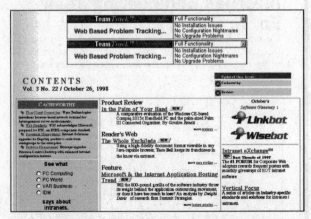

Many companies have their own intranets which can only be accessed by company staff

IP Number

Internet Protocol Number. A number that is used to uniquely identify every computer on the Internet. It takes the following form:

189.104.232.8

Whenever you type in a Web address, the equivalent IP address is looked up in a directory and it is the IP address that is used to locate the relevant computer.

More details on this subject are available in the online version of the HyperGlossary (**http://www.hyperglossary.co.uk**).

IP Number

Internet Protocol Number. A number that is used to uniquely identify every computer on the Internet. It takes the following form:

189.104.232.8

Whenever you type in a web address, the equivalent IP address is looked up in a directory and it is the IP address that is used to locate the relevant computer.

IP numbers may not be the most interesting things to look at, but they still need a mention

IRC

Internet Relay Chat. A well established mechanism for supporting chat forums. Public and private forums are supported.

See also: Chat Forums.

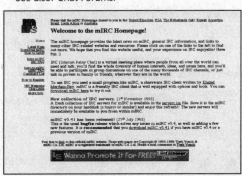

In days gone by IRC was the only way to chat online and it remains popular today

ISDN

Integrated Services Digital Network. A mechanism for using existing telephone lines to provide higher bandwidth communication. Unlike the normal use of telephone lines for transmitting data, there is no need for a modem. The data is transmitted digitally rather than being converted to

For fast access to the Internet get yourself an ISDN line from BT

analogue (and back to digital at the far end). This permits faster connections between computers and faster transmission.

ISP

An Internet service provider is an organisation that offers Internet services including connection to the Internet and Web site hosting. Internet service providers are invariably referred to as ISPs.

For more details on this subject, go along to the online version of the HyperGlossary (**http://www.hyperglossary. co.uk**).

ClaraNET claims to be the UK's most successful independent ISP

Java

Java is a programming language that is used for writing programs that can be downloaded to your computer through the Internet and immediately run within your browser. These programs are called applets. Java is a portable language that runs on any computer supported by a piece of software called the Java Virtual Machine (JVM for short). The popular browsers have a JVM built in and thus are capable of running Java applets.

See also: Applet.

Java is the programming language of choice for many Webmasters

JavaScript

A language that is embedded in Web pages and is executed by the browser as it displays the page. It can be used to make the Web page more dynamic and to validate the data that is typed into forms. Not to be confused with Java – which is a different language.

See also: VBScript.

JavaScript can be used to make Web pages more lively. Just don't use too much of it

JPEG

The Joint Photographic Experts Group (JPEG) format is one of the two standard formats

used for images on the Web. The other is GIF. The JPEG format is well suited for photographic images.

See also: GIF.

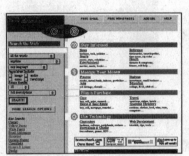

Key Word

A word you type into a search engine to indicate what pages you would like it to locate for you.

Kilobyte

A thousand bytes. The purists will tell you that it is actually the binary equivalent, which is 1024!

See also: Byte, Megabyte, Gigabyte, Terabyte.

Be careful not to get Kilobyte mixed up with Killer Bite – only one of these is fatal!

THE **BIG BOOK** OF
INTERNET ANSWERS

LAN

Local Area Network. A computer network situated within a given locality, typically one building or one site. See also: WAN.

Leased-line

A telephone line connection between two points that is rented for exclusive use by an organisation. The advantage over redialling each time is that you get a consistent quality of line and resulting

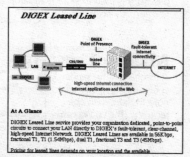

higher speed of data communication. It is usually cheaper when the line is in use for a large percentage of the time.

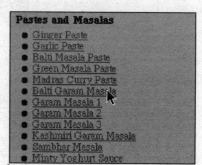

Link

An abbreviation for Hyperlink.

Login/Logon

The process of entering into a computer system is referred to as logging in or logging on. These terms are used most frequently when you have to identify yourself to the computer system by specifying an id and password. The id is a string

A password is a string of characters that only you know, unless you tell someone else

of characters that identifies you, typically your name or initials. The password is a string of characters that only you know. The password is used to stop other people masquerading as you. See also: Id, Password.

Mailing List

A mechanism for sending copies of a single email note to more than one recipient. The copies can be made on the user's machine. Alternatively a single copy is send to a server on the Internet for copying and sending on to the list of recipients. There are thousands of mailing lists operated on the Internet on all imaginable topics.

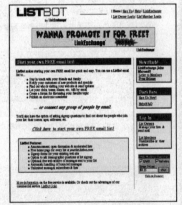

More details on this subject are available in the online version of the HyperGlossary (**http://www.hyperglossary.co.uk**).

Megabyte

A million bytes. The purists will tell you that it is actually the binary equivalent, which is 1024 x 1024!

See also: Byte, Kilobyte, Gigabyte.

MIME

Multipurpose Internet Mail Extensions. The standard used on the Internet for identifying different types of file. It was initially introduced for attaching files to Internet email messages, but is also used by Web servers to inform browsers what type of file they are sending. Examples of MIME types are 'text/html' for standard Web pages and image/jpeg for JPEG files. Recent browsers and email systems handle a large number of MIME types automatically.

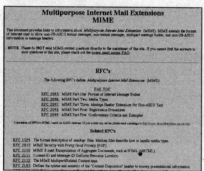

Mirror Sites

A mirror site of a Web site is an exact copy of the original site. They are commonly used for Web and FTP sites when the original site cannot cope with the load that is being put on it. An added benefit can be that one of the mirror sites is more accessible to you and therefore provides faster access.

To ensure you get a fast download go to your nearest site

Modem

Modulator demodulator. A device that is used to transmit data between two computers over a normal telephone line. You have one modem at each end of the phone line. At the sending end the data is converted into an analogue signal so that the telephone system can handle it, and at the receiving end the analogue system is converted back to digital form so that the computer can handle it.

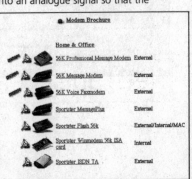

Netiquette

Net etiquette. A set of guidelines on how you should behave when you are communicating over the Internet.

Netizen

Net citizen. Those who spend much of their time on the Internet. Used in the same way as you would talk about the citizens of Paris, for example.

Netscape

The company that is responsible for one of the leading browsers – Navigator and many other Internet products. It was the success of the early version of Navigator that started the rapid growth of the World Wide Web.

Network

Two or more computers connected together so that from one computer you can access data or run software on another computer.

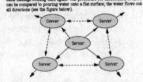

"Pouring water" principle of Usenet News distribution

Network News

An alternative name for Usenet.

Newbie

A person who is new to the Internet.

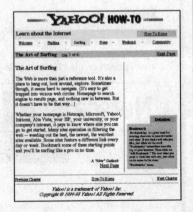

Newsgroup

A discussion group on Usenet.

NNTP

Network News Transport Protocol. The protocol used to support the Usenet service on the Internet. See also: Protocol.

Node

Any single computer on a network. Sometimes also referred to as hosts.

Password

The password is a string of characters that only you know. The password is used to stop other people masquerading as you. Sometimes the computer will check that not only have you typed the correct password in but that each letter is also in the correct case (upper or lower). To be effective,

a password needs to be a string of characters that no one else could guess. So your name, initials, initials in reverse order are not good passwords. Mixing case and adding characters other than letters of the alphabet will help. Something like AZ9%3cG would be quite secure, the only problem being that you have to be able to remember it.

See also: Login.

Plug-in

A browser plug-in is a computer program that adds functionality to the browser. The plug-ins are used to handle file formats that the browser cannot

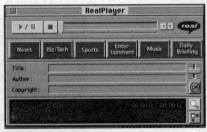

handle itself. The plug-ins in effect become part of the browser, and are more efficient that helper applications.

See also: Helper Applications.

Point of Presence

A location where a you can connect to the Internet or other network, typically via the telephone system. So, if an Internet

Service Provider offers a Point of Presence in London, you will be able to access the Internet by phoning London. Not to be confused with the other POP – post office protocol.

POP

Abbreviation for Point of Presence and for Post Office Protocol. See also: Point of Presence, Post Office Protocol.

more people get on with us

POP is a confusing word – it can stand for Point of Presence or Post Office Protocol. Most ISPs (such as Demon and Direct Connection, shown on this page) will have a Point of Presence that is within local call distance

Portal

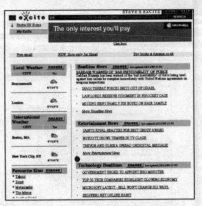

A Web site that sets out to provide a point of entry to the World Wide Web. Examples are Yahoo! and Netscape Netcenter. They provide a wide selection of services (such as free email) and links to the rest of the Web. Their goal is to become your browser home page – the page that appears automatically each time you load your browser, or when you click on the home button.

Post Office Protocol

One of the standard protocols used by your email software when accessing email from the Internet. If your Internet service provider only supports POP, then you will need email software that can handle that protocol. The version number is often tagged on the end. Thus, POP3 is version 3 of the post office protocol.

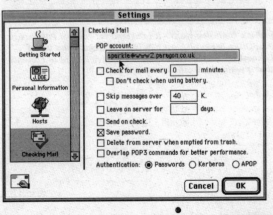

Posting

A message sent to a newsgroup.

See also: Usenet.

Protocol

A language used to communicate between two computer programs. It consists of a set of commands and the rules about how they are used. A major cause of the success of the Internet

has been the widespread adoption of a number of protocols, such as HTTP for communicating with Web Servers, FTP, etc.

Push Technology

A mechanism for sending information to your browser from a Web site at prearranged intervals. You state what information you are interested in and how often you want it updated and the Web site transmits its contents to you accordingly. You do not have to go back and request the latest information. The same technology is referred to as Netcasting by Netscape and Channels by Microsoft.

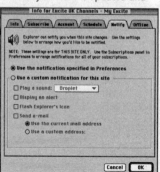

Rendering

The process of displaying a Web page in the browser – displaying the text in the correct size, font and colour, displaying images, etc.

RFC

Request For Comments. RFCs are used to reach agreement on Internet standards. A document (RFC) presenting a proposal for a new standard is published for comments. After taking appropriate actions on the comments a new version of the RFC is published for

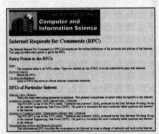

more comments. At some stage it is agreed to go with a particular RFC and those responsible start implementing. Thus an RFC can be a proposal or an agreed standard. There are also RFCs which provide background information on a particular subject. All RFCs can be viewed on the Internet.

Robot

Used to refer to a piece of software that performs a function in the place of a human being. Specifically the search engine tools that surf the Internet looking for pages to add to the search index is sometimes called a robot. The abbreviations bot or Web bot are also used.

Router

A computer at a junction on the Internet that directs data towards its correct destination. They decide which link of the network to send the data based on the IP number of the destination computer.

See also: IP number.

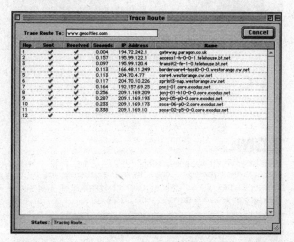

Search Engine

A search engine is a software tool that helps users find Web pages that relate to one or more key words that they have typed in.

More details on this subject are available in the online version of the HyperGlossary (**http://www.hyperglossary.co.uk**).

Server

A computer that provides a service to other computers on the network. For example, a Web server obtains Web pages and other files as requested by a Web user, and sends them to the browser. The term server is also applied to software packages that provide a service – so you also have Web server software, for example. The machines that connect to the server and use the services it offers are known as Client machines.

See also: Client.

SGML

Standard Generalized Markup Language, the international standard for defining descriptions of the structure and content of different types of electronic document. HTML is an example of a description which is defined with SGML.

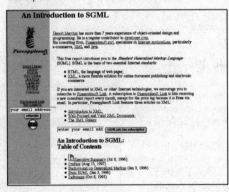

Shareware

Software packages that you can use free of charge for a trial period. After the trial period, you are asked to make a payment. Some packages operate on trust others have logic built into them to stop them working at the end of the trial period. A lot of Internet software is available as shareware.

SMTP

Simple Mail Transport Protocol. The protocol used to send electronic mail over the Internet.

Outgoing Mail Server

Outgoing mail (SMTP) server : www2.paragon.co.uk

Outgoing mail server user name : steveh

Use Secure Socket Layer (SSL) or TLS for outgoing messages :

● Never ◯ If Possible ◯ Always (else fail)

Spam (or Spamming)

The email equivalent of junk mail. The term is used in particular to describe the practice of sending the same message to a number of different Usenet groups or mailing lists. Some groups and mailing lists have rules against spamming, and offenders can get bombarded with flame mail.

An inappropriate attempt to use a mailing list, or USENET or other networked communications facility as if it was a broadcast medium (which it is not) by sending the same message to a large number of people who didn't ask for it. The term probably comes from a famous *Monty Python* skit which featured the word spam repeated over and over. The term may also have come from someone's low opinion of the food product with the same name, which is generally perceived as a generic content-free waste of

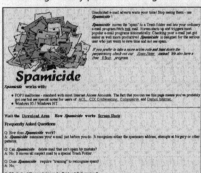

resources. (Spam is a registered trademark of Hormel Corporation, for its processed meat product.)

For example, Mary spammed 50 USENET groups by posting the same message to each. See also: Maillist, USENET.

Spider

A Spider (or Web Crawler) is a piece of software that scans the World Wide Web finding pages to add to the index of a search engine.

See also: Search Engines.

SSL

Secure Sockets Layer. A protocol that supports secure communication over the Internet. SSL supports authentication and encryption. Authentication provides via certificates a means for you to validate who you are in contact with. Encryption codes all the data before it is transmitted, making it impossible for anyone else on the Internet to intercept and read your communications. This is important for shopping on the Web. It

allows you check that the Web site is in fact owned by Dell Computers, and you can send your credit card details without fear that someone else on the Internet will see them. See also: Certificate.

TCP

Part of the TCP/IP suite of protocols used to communicate between machines on the Internet. On the sending computer, TCP splits the data up into manageable sized packets and attaches information such as the

IP number of the target computer. At the receiving computer, it checks all the packets have arrived and issues a request to resend a packet if necessary. When they have all arrived it extracts the data from each packet and assembles it in the correct sequence.

See also: TCP/IP, IP Number.

TCP/IP

Transmission Control Protocol/Internet Protocol. A set of protocols

that are used by computers on the Internet to communicate with each other. It is used by all computers on the Internet or any Intranet.
More details on this subject are available in the online version of the HyperGlossary (**http://www. hyperglossary.co.uk**).

Telnet

An Internet service that allows you to log into a remote computer.

Terabyte

1,000 gigabytes. The purists will tell you that it is actually the binary equivalent which is 1024 x 1024 x 1024 x 1024!
    See also: Byte, Kilobyte, Megabyte, Gigabyte
    UDP.

---

terabyte

A terabyte is a measure of memory capacity and is two to the 40th power or "roughly" (as a decimal number) a thousand billion bytes (that is, a thousand gigabytes).

Also see gigabyte, teraflop, and petabyte.

This term was suggested by Jack Duffie.

URL

Uniform Resource Locator. The mechanism for addressing resources on the Internet. Uniform Resource Locator is invariably abbreviated to URL. The URL is best known for specifying Web addresses. For example, the URL for the New Media in Business Ltd glossary is **http://www.nmib.com/ glossary/index.htm**. This is what you type into the address field in the browser.

More details on this subject are available in the online version of the HyperGlossary (**http://www.hyperglossary.co.uk**).

User Datagram Protocol

One of the protocols for data transfer that is part of the TCP/IP suite of protocols. Unlike TCP, UDP does not check that all the data has been delivered. It is, for example, used for conversations over the Internet where:

1 The human brain will cope with a certain amount of loss of speech.

2 By the time it discovers that some data is lost it will be too late, and

3 The listener will ask the speaker to repeat if he she doesn't understand.

See also: TCP/IP.

```
RFC 768                                                  J. Postel
                                                              ISI
                                                    28 August 1980


                          User Datagram Protocol


    Introduction


    This User Datagram Protocol (UDP) is defined to make available a
    datagram mode of packet-switched computer communication in the
    environment of an interconnected set of computer networks.  This
    protocol assumes that the Internet Protocol (IP) [1] is used as the
    underlying protocol.

    This protocol provides a procedure for application programs to send
    messages to other programs with a minimum of protocol mechanism.  The
    protocol is transaction oriented, and delivery and duplicate protection
    are not guaranteed.  Applications requiring ordered reliable delivery of
    streams of data should use the Transmission Control Protocol (TCP) [2]

    Format

                 0      7 8     15 16     23 24     31
                +--------+--------+--------+--------+
                |     Source      |   Destination   |
                |      Port       |      Port       |
                +--------+--------+--------+--------+
                |     Length      |    Checksum     |
                +--------+--------+--------+--------+
                |
                          data octets
```

Usenet

An Internet service that provides support for newsgroups (or discussion groups) on a large variety of subjects. Each newsgroup consists of a collection of electronic mail messages on a particular subject.

See also: Discussion Group Newsgroup.

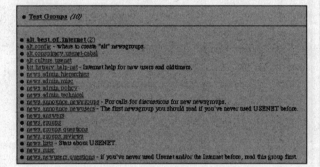

Vaporware/Vapourware

Software products that do not really exist in a usable form. The term was created as a result of the fact that some software companies market products prematurely.

VBScript

Visual Basic Script. A language that is embedded in Web pages and is executed by the browser as it displays the page. It can be used to make the Web page more dynamic and to validate the data that is typed into forms. It serves the same purpose as JavaScript. It is a subset of Visual Basic with one or two additions!

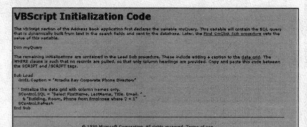

Veronica

A database used to search for particular gopher sites. If you are interested it stands for Very Easy Rodent Oriented Net-wide Index to Computerized Archives.

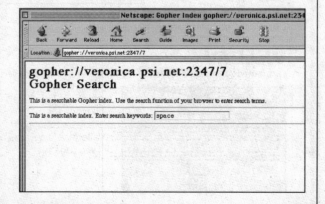

VRML

Virtual Reality Markup Language. A language that is used to create 3D effects on a Web site.

W3C

Abbreviation for World Wide Web Consortium.

WAIS

Wide Area Information Server. A predecessor of the Internet search engines of today.

WebDAV

Distributed Authoring and Versioning on the Web. A proposal from an Internet Engineering Task Force workgroup for a mechanism to support collaborative development of Web pages.

WAN

Wide Area Network – a computer network that is spread over more than one location, e.g. linking offices of a company around the world.

See also: LAN.

Web

Short for World Wide Web. Since the words 'world wide' are omitted, it is equally appropriate for an Intranet and the Internet.

See: World Wide Web.

Webmaster

The person who is responsible for maintaining a Web site. The term Webmaster may be used for both men and women.

Web Page

A document that is stored in HTML format. It can contain text, images and hyperlinks. Web pages are usually grouped with other pages on the same theme to form a Web site.

See also: Web site.

Web Server

A computer that manages a Web site. It passes Web pages to browsers when they request them. The Web pages are often stored on the Web server but could be on another computer on the same network as the Web Server.

Web Site

A collection of Web pages which represent an organisation, individual or subject area. Many companies have their own Web sites, typically containing information on how to contact them and products and services. Each Web site has a home page which is the normal starting point for people visiting the site.

More details on this subject are available in the online version of the HyperGlossary (**http://www.hyperglossary.co.uk**).

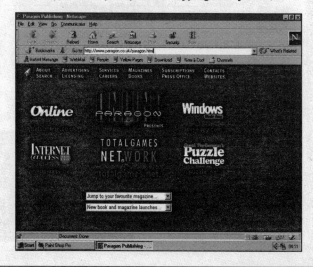

Web Space

The disk space on a Web
Server that is set aside for a
Web site.

World Wide Web

A service that runs on the Internet that allows information to
be stored in a great variety of formats (including text, pictures,
sound and video). It also provides an easy way to link from one
page of information to another simply by pointing with the
mouse and clicking. The World Wide Web is often abbreviated
to WWW or simply the Web.

More details on this subject are available in the online version
of the HyperGlossary (**http://www.hyperglossary.co.uk**).

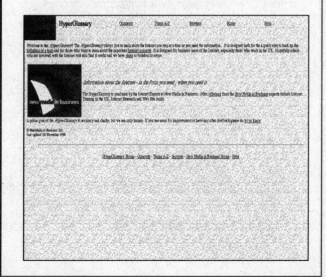

World Wide Web Consortium

The organisation that is responsible for developing the standards (such as HTML and HTTP) that are needed for the World Wide Web. Often abbreviated to W3C.

XML

Extensible Markup Language. A subset of SGML that has been developed for use on the Web, as an alternative to HTML.

XSL

See Extensible Stylesheet Language.

Yahoo!

A popular Web directory. Its Web address is **http:// www.yahoo.com**.

FIFTY TOP SHAREWARE SITES

Whether it's software to create some magic on your home page, or the latest Web utility, these shareware sites are guaranteed to please

Introduction

Y ou don't need to be told again what a wonderful thing the Internet is. Net users will continually extol the virtues of email, the Web and newsgroups, but there is a lot more to it than just that. Amongst other things, it is a paradise for anyone who likes free or cheap software and, let's face it, who doesn't? Whether you want a hardware driver for that archaic soundcard in your PC, a couple of Web utilities, or little software packages which you can use to jazz up the appearance of your computer's desktop, there's a veritable treasure trove of resources to be found on the Web. And the chances are that whatever model of computer you use, there will be software to fit your needs.

Surely, you cry, software will cost lots of dosh regardless of whether it's on the Internet or not. This is not necessarily the case. Although you can buy software over the Net, there is an abundance of free or inexpensive stuff there, too. Most of the software which can be downloaded straight from the Internet can be divided into three categories. The majority of it is 'shareware' which allows you to use the program for nothing during an initial evaluation period, paying a small registration fee if you wish to continue using it. This fee helps with the development of the software and also entitles you to receive information such as fixes for any bugs in the program or announcements about new upgrades. Other software is graded as 'freeware' which is completely free of charge and you can use it as often as you want. Variations on this theme include postcardware – where the author requests a postcard from you if you use it – and emailware.

Additionally, you can get hold of demo versions of many programs or games. These will either be fully working versions of a software package which will only work for a short period of time, or a stripped-down version of a program which gives you a taster of what the real thing is like.

Windows 95.com

http://www.winfiles.com

Platform: Windows 95

Obviously, this is for Windows 95 users only, hence the name of the site. The shareware here includes desktop features, games, multimedia and authoring packages. You can browse the site using the Windows 95 replica interface or by using the powerful search facility which utilises a drop-down menu. As well as shareware there is also a great section for finding drivers for your computer's hardware.

Shareware.com

http://www.shareware.com/

Platform: PC, Mac, Unix, Amiga, Atari

This is the best site for finding shareware for different platforms, from Windows to Amiga to Unix. There are various means of searching for what you require and when you have exhausted what is already on offer, it is always worth going back and checking for new additions. You can also take a look at the pick of the day for Mac or PC. It is probably best to know what you are looking for here but at least there is a good chance you will find it.

Tucows

http://www.tucows.com/

Platform: PC and Mac

Regarded as one of the best shareware sites around, Tucows is
hugely popular. The sheer amount of software available from
Tucows is apparent when you consider that for the Mac, there
are 45 different categories of programs. There is a similar
number for the PC, too. Software here ranges from general

utilities to weather forecasting
applications. The site is easy to
get around and every piece of
software is rated on a scale of
one to five cows.

Info-Mac

http://www.pht.com/info-mac/

Platform: Mac

If you already know what program you want, then this is a
great site for Mac users. It really has got a stack of software.
Info-Mac files are available from umpteen FTP sites around the
globe and this URL takes you to a site that will then direct you
to your closest mirror site. Once on your chosen mirror, you'll
find a list of programs with a brief abstract of what they do.
The hierarchical database makes finding what you need that bit
easier, though. If you already know what you want, simply
enter it into the on-site search box and you're away.

Shareware95.com

http://www.shareware95.com

Platform: Windows 95

This site is for Windows 95 users only and bears more than a passing resemblance to Windows95.com, with a similar interface and similar content. This site is not quite as far-reaching, though, and although it does have a powerful search facility it is not as easy to browse around. There are also hardware drivers and a few tips, making this another useful resource for Windows 95 users.

Shareware Stockpile

http://www.stockpile.com

Platform: PC, Mac

Shareware Stockpile is one of the best sites there is if you are not really sure exactly what you want. The site is very easy to browse, so it is simply a case of choosing which platform you want software for and then having a look through the various different categories to find something you want. Not the biggest collection, but satisfactory nonetheless.

UK Shareware

http://www.ukshareware.com

Platform: Mac, PC

There seem to be a lot more demos on here than actual shareware and it doesn't appear to contain quite as much as some other sites. On a more positive note, though, the software that is available looks to be good so you are less likely to waste time downloading something that's completely useless. When you are just starting out on the hunt for shareware this could be well worth a visit.

Rocket Download

http://www.rocketdownload.com

Platform: PC

The categories here are a little more fun-orientated with features such as action, arcade, kids and music. There's a large collection here and it is very easily to navigate if you use the framed version of the site. The program descriptions are rather on the brief side but there are loads of games and fun utilities for the less serious computer user.

ROCKETDOWNLOAD.COM
Your better choice for downloading.

WinSite

http://www.winsite.com
Platform: PC

WinSite contains a huge amount of software for Windows users and you have the option of browsing the site by different groups. If you already know what you are after, then the powerful search facility should be sufficient to find what you need. There's also a 'hot software' section and a help area. Windows users should get a lot of joy out of this.

32bit.com

http://www.32bit.com
Platform: Windows 95/NT/

This collection of 32-bit applications contains an impressive collection of programs. There is also a discussion forum so you can talk about various shareware issues with people around the world. There's certainly enough here to keep you occupied for some time.

Amiga Freeware/ Shareware Software

http://www.cucug.org/amisoftware.html

Platform: Amiga

The beauty of the Net is its sheer size and because of that it can cater for a diverse audience. In this case, it means that unrepentant Amiga users can also get their fill of software. There isn't a huge range of programs, for the simple reason that more has been written for other computer platforms. Nevertheless, there's enough in the way of Web browsers, utilities, tools and emulators here to keep Amiga users going for a while.

Children's Software

http://www.gamesdomain.com/tigger/sw-kids.html

Platform: PC and Mac

Apparently, "it's wonderful that I can find out what programs appeal (or not) to my children before I pay for them." Whether you are after some fun or educational programs for your young tearaway, or you are secretly looking for something to keep yourself amused, then pay this place a visit. The selections are graded by recommended age so you'll get a good idea of what is suitable for your little terrors.

Download.com

http://headlines.yahoo.com/download/Software

Platform: PC and Mac

It's nice of those nice people at Yahoo! to supply us with a site full of software. You can browse or search (after all, if you can't search properly on a search engine it's time to get worried) and although it doesn't look great, there's a fair amount here to keep you interested. As well as separate sections for Mac and PC software there is also educational content, a games section and a collection of Internet software.

Dr. Shareware

http://www.rbi.com/~salegui/jim/

Platform: Mac

A great site for the PC sceptics, as Dr. Shareware only offers treatment for Apple Mac patients. The Doc does offer a lot of programs from his own site in terms of applications, anti-virus software and games. Almost as important are the hundreds of hotlinks to other download sites for other Apple software and information. If that's not enough, you can link to newsgroups or online catalogues as well.

My Shareware Page

http://www.mysharewarepage.com/

Platform: PC

More sections than you can shake a stick at. If you've got a couple of years to spare you can have a good look at everything here, but you'll probably not get through all of it even then. With brief descriptions and a well-framed interface, this huge database should be checked out if you've got the energy to trawl round it.

JavaShareware

http://www.javashareware.com/

Platform: PC, Mac

Once you've finished decorating your desktop, beefing up your utilities, and playing games to death you might want to get a bit more advanced. If you're into Java, this place has got applets, beans, classes and everything else you need to make it less of a palaver.

JavaShareware.com

Travis' Best PC Shareware Programs

http://www.wsu.edu:8080/~tsolin/share/

Platform: PC

Not the best arranged collection of shareware in the world, but useful nonetheless. The resources are collected into three broad categories but they could do with being divided up a little more stringently. However, if you still haven't found what you are looking for, this is worth a quick browse.

Travis' Best Macintosh Shareware Programs

http://www.wsu.edu:8080/~tsolin/macshare/

Platform: Mac

Obviously a nice bloke, this Travis, because he's put this little lot together to go alongside his PC selection, despite the fact that he doesn't even use a Mac himself. He even apologises if any of the programs he features aren't that good and invites you to let him know if this is the case so he can sort it out. The PC area of the site is at http://www.wsu.edu:8080/~tsolin/share/.

Slaughterhouse

http://www.slaughterhouse.com

Platform: PC

Anybody who rates programs using skeletons has got to be alright, and Slaughterhouse does just that – along with notes, size of file and a description of the program. The drop-down menu offers loads of different categories so you won't have to sift through a multitude of programs before you find what you want.

The ULTIMATE Macintosh

http://www.freepress.com/myee/ultimate_mac.html

Platform: Mac

This is not just a shareware site but a huge archive of information, downloads, columns and everything else of interest for Macintosh addicts around the planet. There are links to other Apple shareware sites as well, so if you want to boost your Mac then a visit to this site will keep you busy for months to come.

Sander's Keyscreen Previewer

http://www.keyscreen.com/

Platform: PC

Although this site doesn't contain the largest amount of shareware on the Internet, it is brilliant in terms of discovering exactly what you are going to get. Not only does it have a description of each package, but there are several screenshots and tutorial-like run-throughs. There's no reason for picking the wrong product after you've visited this place.

SharePaper

http://www.sharepaper.com/

Platform: PC

Not the prettiest site around, but there are lots of software reviews here and a regular SharePaper Newsletter. As well as various applications and games there are links to other resources such as authors and organisations, which means that when you get bored of this site you can find something of similar interest without too much hassle.

The Acorn Cybervillage – Software

http://www.cybervillage.co.uk/acorn/software.stm

Platform: Acorn

Apparently, mighty oaks from little acorns grow. This is not exactly the case with Acorn computers but if you are one of the minority who still swear by them, there are resources for you. Obviously, there isn't going to be as much to interest you as many of the other sites listed here offer Windows 95 users, but anything's certainly better than nothing.

Galt Shareware Zone

http://www.galttech.com/

Platform: PC

A return to the Windows 95-style interface here and this site concentrates a lot on desktop gimmicks. There is a screensaver heaven and also a series of desktop themes which turn your Windows 95 desktop into a shrine for your favourite pop group or film. There are also shareware reviews and recommended downloads, along with information on shareware Cds.

Windows 95 Emporium

http://www.clarityconnect.com/webpages/sjs23/home.html

Platform: Windows 95

Another site for you lucky Windows 95 users. The Windows-style fascia is hardly original and the content is pretty much as expected. If you want to chat about shareware there is a chat room here so you can go and find out what the rest of the world thinks of your latest find before you spend time downloading it.

Clicked.com Top 20 Shareware Gallery

http://www.clicked.com/shareware/

Platform: PC

Not just the top 20 overall shareware programs, but six categories are featured, from graphics to communication, multimedia, Internet and utilities. If you are happy to let others tell you what you should have on your machine rather than hunt round the Net to find what you need, this could be the place to fulfil your shareware desires.

Aminet

http://wuarchive.wustl.edu/pub/aminet/info/www/

Platform: Amiga

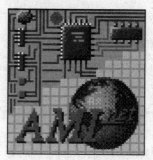

A site for Amiga aficionados, Aminet looks like your average FTP site with dull grey backgrounds and various subdirectories. More importantly, there are loads of programs to download, whether you are after business applications, musical software or something to improve your graphics. Definitely worth a visit for Amiga owners.

The Mac Software Catalog

http://www.nexor.com/public/mac/archive/welcome.html

Platform: Mac

A haven of Mac software, whether you are after the latest in gaming shoot 'em ups or a couple of System Extensions. You can either browse through at your leisure or search for something specific. There is also help on how to download the files and an explanation of what the different file extensions mean, so you've got a good idea of what you are actually downloading.

The Mac Software Catalog

University of Texas Mac Archive

http://wwwhost.ots.utexas.edu/mac/main.html

Platform: Mac

Again, this is for the Mac lovers and it boasts formidable resources. These can be searched via three different indexes: either by author, date or product. Alternatively, you can browse through the various diverse types of files available. These include 21 different options from anti-virus software to utilities. Easily enough for most Apple users.

Freeware 95

http://www.geocities.com/SiliconValley/Lakes/1712/

Platform: Windows 95

Everything's completely free on this Web site so you can download to your heart's content without having to worry about paying a load of registration fees. This place doesn't have a great deal of practical applications, but for the gizmo lovers it will be a paradise. There's a plethora of desktop wallpapers, themes and screensavers for your Windows 95 PC. Other sections include more interesting utilities, games and tools.

Shareware Village

http://www3.sympatico.ca/ken.macdonald/Shareware/shareware.html

Platform: Windows 95

This place falls in with the better looking shareware sites around. Fun stuff comes up with everything from educational games to screensavers and the utilities section offers you a choice of automation tools, file managers or any number of useful programs to use on your PC. Very handy and easy to use, too.

The Best Free Internet Software

http://www.afn.org/~afn45694/

Platform: PC

If you are more concerned with improving your Internet experience than playing games or jazzing up your desktop, then this is the place to come. Whether it's email programs or an HTML reference library, everything on this Web site is completely free so you don't even have to pay any shareware fees. Sort out all things Internet from here.

Shareware from STAR

http://shareware.org/

Platform: PC

This site is well split up into various sections, which means that if you have a general idea of what you might be after, this place should be able to help. If you already know the name of the program you want, then the search engine should sort you out. To keep up with the latest products you can check out what's new this week, whether it's for Windows 95, Windows 3.x or MS-DOS.

Jumbo Shareware

http://www.jumbo.com

Platform: PC, Mac

Jumbo is by no means an exaggeration where this site is
concerned. Navigation is quite easy as the site is split into
channels, whether it's homework, Internet stuff or entertainment.
When you have accessed a particular channel there are various
sub-channels, such as the Quake channel on Games. There's an
abundance of shareware, freeware and demos here so take a
look – you won't be disappointed.

The CAVERN'S Windows 95 Page

http://www.aiag.net/~mgoetz/win95.html

Platform: Windows 95

It seems that Windows 95 users enjoy helping each other without
helping out their less fortunate Windows 3.x relations, and this is
another site to help the Win95 crew. It covers many areas such as
Net software, utilities, and miscellaneous files, such as
screensavers. There is also a tips and tricks section to help you get
the most out of your PC.

Easy Software

http://ourworld.compuserve.com/
homepages/easysoftware/

Platform: PC

There isn't a huge amount of shareware on this site – indeed, the choice is quite limited because the programs are all from the one supplier. Nevertheless, there are some useful little bits here to make your life on the PC a little bit easier. Most of it is there to simplify common procedures – hence the name of the site.

Freeware Favorites

http://www.webdesigns1.com/freeware/

Platform: PC

Freeware Favorites is actually more of an online magazine than a software archive. There are nine issues available at the moment – and each one includes three or four different free programs. There are reviews, screenshots and links to the relevant site so you can go and download it if you want to. It's nice to have some idea of what you are getting before wasting your time and money downloading.

Game Shack

http://www.jorsm.com/~dbrtos/

Platform: PC

If you can't be bothered finding software of practical use and just want to have some fun playing a few games then cut straight to this Web site which concentrates on just that. The size of the collection is a little disappointing, but at least all you have to do is click on your chosen operating system before looking through at your leisure.

Pass the Shareware

http://www.passtheshareware.com

Platform: PC, Mac, Unix

A great place to find shareware because if this place doesn't have what you are looking for there are links to loads of other sites. If that's not enough, there are various other sections with information on shareware companies, resources for shareware authors and general information. Great place to learn about and get hold of software.

Shareware Junkies.com

http://www.sharewarejunkies.com

Platform: PC, Mac

This really is the place for shareware addicts with a well-designed and easy-to-use site. What's more, this is not just a case of downloading with only a vague idea of what you are going to get. There is full information on all the programs along with reviews. Visit once and we dare you to stay away.

File Mine

http://www.filemine.com

Platform: Mac, PC, Unix

There's a really useful search facility here or you can have a look through the games, home, Internet, multimedia, programs or demos sections to see if anything takes your fancy. There's also an interesting survey being carried out on what motivates people to register their shareware – it's because we're all responsible Net users, of course.

Microsoft Windows Family

http://www.microsoft.com/windows/

Platform: Windows 95, NT

Yes, that small cottage industry that is Microsoft has one or two things on offer which may be of interest. There's a lot more here than just shareware and freeware, but if you're a dedicated PC lover, then this place is bound to be of interest in many ways.

My Desktop

http://www.mydesktop.com

Platform: PC

Everything you need to keep your desktop happy can be found on this site. There are little toolbar utilities and the like to help you make the most of your limited desktop space, but also loads of other software. Each program has a short description along with screenshots and operating system information.

Nonags
http://nonags.com/nonags/main.html
Platform: Windows 95/NT

Split loosely into Internet applications and general applications, this site then has loads of sub-directories which makes it quite easy to find what you want. To keep up-to-date there's a What's New section so you'll always be in touch with the latest news. It's all free as well.

Stroud's Consumate Internet Apps List
http://cws.internet.com
Platform: PC

Apparently the place to find the latest and greatest software on the Internet, there's a decent range of freeware and shareware here. It's well designed and easy to get around with a Top Twenty chart, search engine and loads of different software reviews so you know whether what's featured is actually any good.

Windows 95
and Mac Joke Wallpaper

http://www.jokewallpaper.com/

Platform: Windows 95, Mac

Not, strictly speaking, a shareware Web site but if you want to jazz up your computer's desktop display, whether on a PC or a Mac, then this is the place to come. There are all manner of humourous JPEG images here which you can have as your wallpaper, start-up or shut-down screens, and if you are not sure what to do with them when you've found them, there's a FAQ section to help.

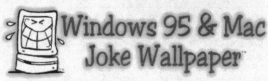

No Shirt.   No Shoes.   No Problem.

Netscape Home Page

http://home.netscape.com

Platform: PC, Mac

This site doesn't just have Netscape's ubiquitous Web browser, but various other programs, plug-ins and browser add-ons which come in useful. If you use the Netscape browser, call in here from time to time for product news and extra pieces of software. Currently, the new fangled Netscape Communicator is available for download.

PCWin Resource Center Home Page

http://www.pcwin.com

Platform: PC

This is a simple Web site which doesn't overload you with options and information. It essentially offers easy to understand help on installing your downloads, a few tips and a satisfactory amount of software for you to enjoy. Definitely worth a visit if you're a member of the PC posse.

Shareware Shop

http://www.bsoftware.com/share.htm

Platform: PC, Mac

A brilliant site which doesn't just contain huge amounts of programs (more than 50,000 listings!), but has featured shareware, links, a tour of the site, reviews, ads, author network and much more. Not just a place for finding the stuff but an excellent resource for users and authors alike.

Shareware Central

http://www.q-d.com/swc.htm

Platform: PC

A slightly different approach to finding yourself some shareware and very much in the concept's best traditions. The descriptions of the programs are written by the authors themselves. And just to make sure you get to send your feedback, there is an email link to the author from the site. Nice to see something with a little bit of originality.

The Shareware Story

Shareware was born simultaneously in two places. In Tiburon, California it was born as the program PC-Talk, fathered by Andrew Fluegelman. In Bellevue, Washington, it sprang to life as PC-File® , the brain child of Jim Knopf. This is my half of the story.

I'm Jim Knopf, the father of Shareware. This is the story which I used to call "How did I get into this mess?" I wrote it in 1987.

A note on file compression

Any half-decent piece of software will be a considerable size, and getting all the data transferred over the Internet and through your modem can take a substantial amount of time. Everyone is aware of how long it can sometimes take for a few pictures to appear on a Web browser, so just think how long it could take for a piece of software to get through to your modem. In order to make the transfer of files over the Net quicker and more efficient, most are compressed into single files, or in the case of really large programs, several files, which are called archives. The archives take up less space and therefore take less time to download. The programs in their compressed state cannot be used as they are, so before making use of them you have to decompress the files. In many cases the software comes as a 'self-extracting archive' which means it will automatically expand to its original state as soon as you download it (occasionally you have to double-click the downloaded program icon). If this is not the case, then you will need to decompress the files yourself. There are several programs which will expand the software and reverse this process of compression. Of the various programs around which can decompress downloaded files we recommend the following ones:

StuffIt Expander

This is a freeware product for Macintosh, Windows or DOS users, which can expand most types of files found online. Using the program is simple. When you have downloaded StuffIt, install it on your hard drive (obviously StuffIt itself is not compressed, otherwise you might be in a bit of trouble). You can then configure your Web browser, via its preferences, to automatically launch StuffIt whenever you download a file. Alternatively, you can use the application as a 'drag and drop' facility. Whenever you download a file you will be asked where you want to save it. Save it on to your desktop and then simply drag the file on to the StuffIt icon and it will get to work for you. It's free, you can get it from **http://www.aladdinsys.com** and it's available for Mac and PC.

WinZip

WinZip is a shareware product for Windows users which, like StuffIt, can expand most of the file types you will find on the Web. WinZip is more user-friendly than StuffIt and comes with a Wizard that will take you through the easy process of unzipping files and placing them where you want on your hard drive. Again, WinZip will detect your Web browsers and automatically launch when you download a file. Alternatively, there is a drag and drop facility. WinZip costs $29, from **http://www.winzip.com** and is available for the PC.

Share and share alike

The concept of shareware originated in the US over 15 years ago in 1981. Amazingly enough, it was developed in two different places simultaneously. One of the programs concerned was a database package which programmer Jim Knopf shared with some of his friends as they began to build their own computers. His friends then shared it with their friends and so the program became more and more popular. This presented its own problems for Jim who always tried to keep users updated with fixes and updates. This became an expensive and time-consuming pastime, so Jim needed a way of knowing which users were the serious ones and would, therefore, benefit from the regular updates. As a result of this, a message was included in the program to the effect that users should continue to share the program, but that those who wished to be placed on the mailing list should send a voluntary donation of $10.

In a remarkable coincidence, it turned out that another programmer, Andrew Fluegelman, was doing almost exactly the same thing and the concept of shareware was born.

From those humble beginnings, shareware has grown into a huge industry, with thousands of programs now available for the payment of a nominal fee. The advantages of the idea are obvious: shareware programs go to the opposite extreme of most software packages which have stringent rules about copyright. Here, the opposite applies – computer users are actively encouraged to copy and distribute the software. Most commercial programs will set you back a fair few quid, whereas shareware is available for a comparatively low fee.

Take note, however, that the reason shareware works is because of the number of people who pay their registration fees. If you do download a shareware program, by all means use it for a few days to see if you like it, but if you are going to continue, then pay the fee. It's hardly going to make you bankrupt and unless everyone pays their shareware fees, the programmers will stop writing. Come on, cough up – it won't break the bank!

For more on the history of shareware and other information, visit Jim Knopf's home page at **http://www.halcyon. com/knopf/jim**.

Top ten shareware tips

● Pick and choose carefully. It's easy to go overboard and fill your hard drive with programs you will never use.

● Make a note of what you download and which directories it is saved to. Otherwise you'll forget what you have downloaded and then wonder why you have no space left on your hard drive.

● Don't expect everything you download to be perfectly programmed. There's always an element of a risk involved with shareware developed by amateur programmers.

● Pay your shareware fees to ensure that people continue to write it!

● Keep the 'Read Me' files, or print them out. You may need to refer to them at a later date. There's nothing more infuriating than trashing everything except the application and then realising that you need to check how it works.

● Get a virus protector! No, really. Don't download without one. For more information check out the feature on page 16.

● Remember that the bigger the file, the more you'll pay in phone charges getting it. Is it really worth having a heart attack when you receive your BT bill just to get hold of a Boyzone screensaver?

● It's often possible to get the software by other means. Many magazines have covermounted CD-ROMs containing shareware, saving the hassle of download.

● Be wary of beta release software. This is software which is not completely developed and may contain various bugs.

● For faster downloads, pick the time and place. Download from sites in the UK or European mirror sites, and try to get stuff in the morning, before much of the US wakes up (and the Net slows down).